Laura De La Cruz
75 County Road A074
Chaparral, NM 88081
915-603-0209
Thetakepen@gmail.com

Aussie Herding
Interviews with Top Australian Shepherd Stockdog Trainers

by Laura De La Cruz, ed.

Thank you for purchasing this book. It has been a real joy working on this project. Let me tell you how this all came about.

I live in Southern New Mexico where I have a small training facility. I offer herding, rally and obedience training. I love herding, having been involved since 2005 when I started with my first Border Collie and my first Aussie. I've come a long way since then, moving from the city to the country, getting my own stock, becoming a trainer, becoming an AKC and AHBA herding judge, all thanks to this addiction we call herding!

One day, while unpacking, I came across my box of herding books and DVDs. I found my copy of "Top Trainers Talk about Starting a Sheepdog: Training a Border Collie on Sheep and Other Livestock" by Molloy and Nadelman. I was struck by the thought that it would be pretty cool to have a similar book, talking about training Australian Shepherds.

So I did what anyone else in the 21st century would do, I went on Facebook and asked people to give me recommendations for trainers to interview. Some of those people are in this book. There are others that were unable to participate at this time, due to time constraints and/or personal circumstances. For that reason, I'm calling this book "Volume One" in hopes of getting participation for a second and maybe a third book.

I would like to thank those who participated in this book. Reading their interviews was not only fascinating, but educational! I had a blast learning from the experts and I hope you do as well.

You may have noticed that this book has a different cover than the eBook. This is because it is slightly different. The pictures of the contributors have been deleted here due to formatting issues.

Thanks also to my friends at Take Pen Herding, particularly Joan Morgan, who takes care of things when I go off to trial and judge.

This book is dedicated to all my Aussies, but especially Itsy (Odyssey's De La Cruz, OTDs, STDdc, CD, RE, CGC, TDI), my first!

Laura De La Cruz
thetakepen@gmail.com
915-603-0209

ELSIE RHODES

Located in beautiful Winlock, WA, Elsie offers herding lessons, clinics and dog training. Elsie began herding in 1976 and has been active ever since! Elise was an AKC and ASCA judge, but now focuses her time primarily on training and trialing. She does judge AHBA trials at her place in Washington State.

To contact Elise:

Elrhodes2@msn.com

360-785-0831

How long have you been involved in training and trialing Aussies? How did that involvement come about?

I was raised on a small farm, ranch whatever you want to call it, only 125 acres. We had dairy cattle, goats, pigs, horses, ducks, chickens, cats and of course we had dogs, including Aussies. Animals of one type or another have been a part of my life since childhood. Being a typical girl horses were my main interest and I spent many happy hours riding and training them

Our dogs were all breeds, shapes and sizes. Some were pure bred, others mixes. We didn't necessarily train our dogs to work livestock but we did have dogs that knew when milking time was and headed out to escort the cows into the barn. These were self-trained dogs who learned by doing chores with us.

When we didn't have that type of dog around, or we were doing something other than taking the animals to the barn, my four siblings and I did the herding. Our cattle seemed to delight in escaping which provided hours of, I guess you could call it, entertainment. If we had to move them to different pastures or load them for hauling the five of us could spend hours chasing cattle about while our dad dictated where he thought we should be to get them where he wanted them. BTW, my Dad's commands were far more colorful than what you hear in the trial arena.

Because of this background I think I can safely say I've been into herding for well over 65 years. That number is allowing me to grow up a bit before I began actually moving stock. The experience of moving stock as a child has been a great asset. I have a basic understanding of stock, plus tons of experience moving them myself.

Herding with dogs come into my awareness at the ASC of WA meetings in 1976. Looking back I realize there was much talk but not much real knowledge. That is OK; we all started on the same page. In fact we didn't know anything except that Aussies were for herding.

Club members were excited and looking for opportunities to try our dogs. One member arranged for us to go to a ranch that had Scottish Highlander cattle. They grouped up in a tight circle, heads out or was it in, so long ago I'm a bit fuzzy, daring any dog to try to get to them. The Highlanders won. (A few months ago I put all my ASC of WA Aussie Prints into the recycling bin. Wish I had them now so I could give you names and dates.) A group of us loaded up our dogs and went to Canada where we watched and learned from a fantastic Border Collie man. Someone found sheep and we spent an afternoon working them, we had far more success than with the Highlanders.

Time moved on, I did find locations to train my Aussie. At last the day came when I ran in my first trial. What I am going to copy here is from something I wrote a while ago about trialing. I can't do a better job than this to explain about trialing then and today.

"My records are a bit weak, so I couldn't find the exact year for the first trial I entered. It was in 77 or 78. It was in July in Roy, Washington on ducks. Oby Blanchard was our judge and Wally Butler was the apprentice. I was the timer until my run.

I walked into the arena, my mouth dried out. My tongue stuck to the roof of my mouth. I could not say a word. I was shaking. I don't remember a lot about the run. I do remember that following my run I was still shaking so hard they had to get someone else to run the stopwatch. The tremors were so extreme I couldn't hit the start and stop button.

I still get dry mouth - I chew gum to help with this problem. I still shake but have managed to keep that to a moderate tremble. I must stop off at the bathroom before my run. Each and every trial I find myself wondering, "Why am I doing something that gives me diarrhea, makes me chew gum - which I hate - and makes my insides quiver?"

Where did you get your first Aussie?

My sons, Richard & Michael, wanted a dog. They were both in 4-H and neither was enjoying training our poodle. One of the dogs in the class was an Aussie. Alan Scott owned Sky, a blue merle with blue eyes. Alan's Mother, Joyce Scott Zane, told me about a litter of puppies he had sired. The breeder was Karen Myers. (I don't know where Karen is now and I pretty sure she isn't into Aussies any longer. However, she produced many litters in the 70 and early 80s.) I remembered, from my childhood, that Aussies were fun. We decided to see the litter, maybe there would be a puppy for us. Of course, we came home with a fluffy, blue merle, blue-eyed fellow. He was 10 weeks old when we bought him on the installment plan of 15 bucks down and two monthly payments of $10. That was in 1975.

How did you first hear about the breed?

Growing up we had Aussies. One particular bitch I fondly remember we called Heidi. We named her that because she was shy and always hiding from strangers. Later in life my father and I did breed purebred Aussies but not at that time. We had a lovely Samoyed with the original name of Sam. He and Heidi had several litters. Heidi was a natural bob tail and every one of her pups arrived tailless, fabulously fluffy and beyond imagination cute! Oh yes, she was black, so were all her puppies. They looked like fluffy little black bears.

What makes the Aussie different from other dogs that work stock?

This is such a challenging question. In return I ask you this, have you listened to the wind blowing through the trees? Have you listened enough to know that it sounds one way as it sweeps through a maple, another as it blows about a cedar, a grove of aspen whispers yet another song, and firs have their very own melody? I know the sound some trees made in the wind but can I describe the difference? No. That is truly impossible for me. I feel this question about Aussies is similar; it isn't one I can answer. Yet like the trees in the wind, Aussies have...what is it...uniqueness.

I train all breeds of herding dogs so I have lived with a wide variety of dogs from the Herding group. I find most are more similar than different. Being with their person is far better than being locked away. They have a great eagerness to do things and be active. Some are team players, others not so much; some would rather work on their own. Thinkers, oh yes, and they can problem solve, which can mean they can get out of crates, kennels or yards among other creative activities we may not appreciate.

Is it the Aussie temperament or looks that makes the Aussie special?

I love the way Aussies look. They carry themselves so proud and that cute, cute fluffy butt. I like the no tail; I hope that our government doesn't make that go away. Their look is special.

We have a wide range in temperament within our breed. I don't think there is one thing that says, "This particular temperament or attitude is found in all Aussies." I've had Aussies that could protect a 100 dollar bill in the back of a truck. One of the Aussies I have now (my dear Pert) would pick it up and give it away, especially if there was food involved.

The line of Aussies I own now are, consistently, the most biddable dogs with which I have ever shared my life. Biddable is more than a dog that is versatile. Biddable is a dog that wants to learn and is easily trained; it is so rewarding to have a dedicated partner.

The one thing I wish stood out and shouted I'm an Aussie would be working instinct. Not that I'd want all to have one style or another but I'd love if all of them worked.

What do you look for in a puppy? What do you consider the ideal pup?

Selecting a puppy is not too challenging for me nor will my approach be helpful to others. If I have the opportunity to visit the litter often as it grows, I take the one that picks me. I think they are far more intuitive than I. If I can't visit with a litter I go by what I like to see. I have a thing for black dogs. So my normal request is for a black male. Then I take whatever gets selected for me. It doesn't matter what one I get I'll do the best I can with it.

What do you consider the ideal age for starting a pup on stock? Do you start on sheep? Do you ever use any other stock, like ducks or goats, to start your pups?

I like to expose my own puppies to stock monthly as they grow up. The first stock I take them to is ducks. About the time they think eating ducks is fun I switch to either sheep or goats. When puppies are about 4 months old I like to take them to my flock of sheep, turn them loose and watch. It is always an education as they figure things out. I learn a lot by watching and reading what they do at this age, when they are being allowed to think on their own.

Beginning real training on livestock depends entirely on the individual. Some dogs are ready sooner than others. I start my young dogs when they are both physically and mentally ready. I use the monthly exposure to livestock to help me assess if they are ready. I think they should be physically able to keep up with the stock they will be working. They need to be mentally mature enough to receive praise and/or corrections without falling apart.

How do you raise your Aussies? Are they house dogs or kennel dogs?

All our dogs are house dogs. That doesn't mean they don't spend time outside in yards or kennels but when we are in the house there are dogs around. Our dogs are our family. Dogs that come here for training also are kept in the house and like our dogs do spend some time during the day in runs or yards.

Mr. Man was different. He did not enjoy being in the house during the day. He wanted outside so he could survey all the farm activities. We brought him inside in the evening, our idea not his. At night he always slept against the bedroom door or in a motel at the exit door. Unless he was in a crate I never saw him sleep anywhere else. Man was never a house dog, his choice not ours.

Our dear Frog the Dog, Frog for short, constantly had to be wherever Jim was working, sitting or sleeping. When Jim was in the kitchen the show was so funny and entertaining plus it went on night after night. Frog would walk in then lay down in the middle of the kitchen. Jim would head for the refrigerator or the sink or whatever; there Frog would be laying in the way. Jim would send Frog out of the kitchen. Frog would dutifully get up, go out, turn around, walking right back in and laying down in the middle of the kitchen, exactly where he had been seconds before, the minute Jim was busy. This show went on repeatedly every evening, night after night. It was a never ending scorch of amusement for me. When he left us not having the evening ritual to listen to and watch was the most difficult time for months.

I could go on and on with short stories about sharing our home with each of our dogs, so many in the past 39 years, but of course that isn't the point of this interview. Suffice it to say, each dog has been an individual, each brought their own personality and character which has given me great joy, happiness, laughter, frustration, and even tears. Lucky me, I've had Aussies to enrich my life.

How important is the relationship between an Aussie and its person?

A good solid relationship is the primary element that makes a great dog and handler team. I like my dogs, even the ones in for training, to be totally into me and respect me as the boss. I think it is important that they care how I feel about things and how I respond to situations. The more time they spend with me they more they know what to expect.

Developing a good relationship means I must know my dog too. Each dog is unique, their likes, dislikes, where, what and how they excel. I want to find what turns them on so I can use it as a reward. I need to know the level of correction too, so I won't over or under correct. I feel that training helps to build a relationship, especially with a dog that will be used in competition. Training tricks can be as important to building a relationship as any other training. This is all about developing a team relationship, building our ability to read one another and respect our individuality.

Do you let your pups follow you around when you are doing chores?

I do let puppies follow me around until they decide to help too much. If, when they help, they are following the chore dog's routine and helping him they can continue to come out with me. It they decide to be more creative their chore days have ended until they are older.

When do you like a pup to show interest in stock? Does it matter? Is there an age where you would start to worry if you hadn't seen any interest yet?

I had one dog not go to work until he was about 13 months old. Much older than that I'd be worried. We have far too many Aussies with little or no instinct. If I had a non-worker that dog would be out of the breeding program. I feel we need to be far more selective with our breeding programs; dogs that don't work don't get bred. LOL. That is a dream. It will never happen; maybe with the working fancy but never the conformation people.

Is there an age when an Aussie is too old to start on stock?

I guess if the Aussie was exhibiting unsoundness it would be too old. I'd train any Aussie regardless of it age as long as I knew it was healthy. Over the years older dogs have come to me and if they have instinct they are delighted to do herding. With the older fellows I am more careful to keep them with safe animals but they can learn everything they need to know.

What sort of stock do you use in the beginning? How many?

The beginning...? Guess I am not sure what the beginning is... Are you talking about the puppy I am exposing, as I said I use ducks for the first couple of times as few as five as many as 40 or 50. If we are talking about students I use heavy, well dog broke stock. Over the years that has been ducks, sheep and lately I have been using goats. I like three to five head although I sometimes use up to ten.

Do you use a round pen? If so, at what point in training?

My round pen's diameter is 66 feet; that is where I start all my dogs. I don't think I'd like it much smaller; perhaps it could be a bit bigger but not much. I want to be able to get there if my ducks, sheep or goats need protecting. With dogs in the beginning stages of training protection is sometimes necessary. I feel the round shape helps the dog learn to hold that nice round movement. The round pen seems to let them flow.

Long ago I saw how fences push on dogs. I have played with this idea. I've moved dogs around in a square pens, rectangles and round. I feel like I get nicer movement during those early hours of training when I begin in the round pen. I want the dog to work out at the fence. When I practice walk-up we do it across the round pen not using its circumference. From the beginning I like my dogs to learn to move stock in straight lines, following the fence line in a round pen would not be a straight line.

Often when I am beginning a new lesson I take them back to the round pen. It excites most of my dogs because they have learned that we will be doing something different.

Do you ever use an older dog to help with training? If so, in what way and for how long?

I enjoy having an older and more experienced dog around while I am giving lessons and training. I do believe that one dog can and does learn from another. With that in mind I make sure the extra dog actually knows what he is doing. I do not want to show the inexperienced dog the wrong way to accomplish a task.

I have one of the best dogs I've ever had for helping dogs learn, her name is Pert. She reads all situations well. If the dog in training has it all under control Pert lays around watching. If the dog needs help Pert is there. I normally don't have to tell her to help, she knows. The other thing I like is once the dog in training has things back under control, with Pert's help, she fades out of the picture on her own.

How long? Well, if I am training something and I have a dog that does it extremely well and there is no competition between dogs, I'll let the experienced Aussie help until the new dog learns the job. Then we can move on without help.

What do you like pups/dogs to know before you introduce them to stock? Do you teach any commands off stock?

I like dogs to know how to learn. I think that is a skill in itself. The day puppies come to our home I begin training. I think training and doing things together helps build our relationship. What I train is of less important than the learning experience itself. My dogs learn all the around the house rules important to being part of the family. I also teach lots of tricks, as well as the normal commands, come, sit, down, back, and let me pass through gates first. I have found a puppy's capacity to learn is at its highest from about 4 weeks to 18 weeks. I like to pour information into them.

When I was doing some breeding I loved training the puppies as soon as I could. Feeding time was always a learning time. It is totally amazing what you can train one of those cuties. If you have the time you can have them sitting, standing and downing on command by 6 or 7 weeks. I also worked on house breaking. As soon as they were walking and would awake I would head them for the door. At first there were potty puddles, lots of them. Each time there would be fewer until they could make it out the door to the potty area. I also did crate training with each one.

Do you ever use any tools when training, like a long line or a stock stick?

Oh yes, I use the tool that works best for the dog; stock stick, paddle, boogie bag, and a rock or water filled bottle. Of course my body is a very important tool helping them to do the things I want. I have used a long line too; it certainly can have its place.

What do you like to see in an Aussie in its first few sessions on stock? What would tell you that it is a good prospect?

I like them to circle their stock, trying to keep it together and hit balance to bring the stock to me. I'm really interested in their attitude, I don't like them to be working for themselves, I want them to be aware of me and working for me.

"What would tell you that it is a good prospect?" That is a difficult question. The dog that is good prospect for one person may not be for another. I see lots of dogs that are really nice. But that doesn't mean they are a good prospect for a dog I want to own. A good prospect for me is extremely intense, stops circling on its own within a few minutes and grabs hold of balance. The dogs I like seem to make me feel comfortable.

Can you describe the best pup you ever started? What made it special and where is it today?

I have two great dogs in my life and a third one coming on. Mr. Man is absolutely the best team mate I have ever trained, or did he train me? When it came time to start Man I was ill and off work. He was the very best medication in my life. When I was feeling bad I'd make myself get Man, go to the field and train. It was amazing; I'd totally focus on us until everything else went away. Man got trained every day for the six months it took me to recover, often up to seven times in a day. He was so patent and devoted; he gave me his all from the first work in the morning until the last practice at night, day after day. I always came away feeling better than if I took a hand full of pills. It didn't last as long as pills but when it got bad I would get Man, out we would go again.

What a partner, we were in total harmony, everything was in sync. He could be naughty but that would be the exception not the rule. I was very proud to be his partner at the 2003 ASCA National in Wisconsin where he won the stockdog finals on sheep, ducks and combined. He was the runner up on cattle missing that by 10 points.

Where is he today; he has crossed over the bridge, he left us a 7-21-12. He was 14. How I miss him. Man was such a great dog and my relationship with him was important to me.

Pert is 12 now and my heart is wrapped around her. She is everything to me. While her brother Man was perfect, Pert is an expert and always has her own idea and opinion about everything. (Remember this. Be careful what you name our dog, Pert – Vest's Bell Star Xpert.) We argue a lot as we do jobs around the place, her way or my way; it's been that way from the beginning and is still that way today. (In trials we never argue, she loves to trial, she loves to nail obstacle after obstacle. She remembers courses and since we trial in AKC on three entirely different type courses, AHBA multiple courses there too, and only enough ASCA to get her WTCH, PATDsc, AFTDs,RTDsc, that is a lot to remember. Our brains become as one, doesn't matter if it is her way or mine; we know when to let the other takeover.) I have her with me almost everywhere I go. She is my chore dog, when my grandchildren are here my babysitter, she greets all my guests, and she helps train all my dogs and my student's dogs. As a trialing dog she has been outstanding earning three Working or Herding Championships in ASCA, AHBA and AKC. We have many HIT and High Combined awards. In AKC she is the 2nd dog to earn the advanced title on all stocks and courses. As of today no other dog has accomplish this, just the two of them in over 20 years. It wasn't an easy thing. At 12 she still goes to the barn daily and helps me with my students. She is my heart dog.

Hankie, he is a silly boy. Hank is a Man son. He will be a fine trial dog. He has already earned several HITs and a High Combined. I ran him in a French course where he earned the excellent rating. Hank is still young. We have lots of time to enjoy our journey together.

Tell us a little about your training style. How often do you work a started dog? What skills do you like to train first? When do you move on to the next skill?

One of my main goals is to help the dog learn to leave square. I like it even better if they will widen a bit when they leave on a flank. I am helping them to learn, drive or fetch, doesn't matter, be square. I feel that from the very first exposure to stock square flanks should become a habit. I don't want poor flanking habits to develop. Fetching or driving a flank is a flank and it is square.

When they first meet ducks, as a young pup, I take a large plastic leaf rake with me. As the puppy gets close to the ducks I put it in front of them. In an effort to get to the ducks they turn to go around the rake. They have accomplished their first square flank.

I count training in hours rather than how many times I go out. For beginning dogs I like to work no more than 15 minutes or less per session. As soon as I get what I want I stop. I make sure my dog knows he is a good boy and that I am happy. I feel stopping when they have performed an exercise well gives my dogs more of an idea of what I want. When they think about their lesson the last thing we did is an exercise they did well. I will bring them back three or four times in a day. I train them three or four days a week.

I introduce standing stops from the very first real training period. Once the dog is stopping well I will add the down. Often I add the down when the dog is already standing feeling that instead of fighting with his instinct to get around or move stock; I should take advantage of the standing stop to introduce the down. It seems to work well. As the dogs' training progresses, I make both the stand and the down more difficult by asking for it in various locations other than balance. The end result should be I can stop my dog with either a stand or a down, regardless of what the stock is doing. That doesn't happen overnight it is a building process.

Once I feel my dogs understand all the word commands we move out of the round pen. Since each dog has his own learning curve there is no one amount of time they spend there. I will throw these figures out there, between 30 and 40 hours it all depends on the dog.

Now it is fun to put all these words to use. I like to begin doing jobs and various exercises. I find it gives commands a real meaning when connected to a job or accomplishing a particular task. I have my dogs do all sorts of things including helping me with my lessons as well as helping with the chores.

I don't normally have courses set up but I always have a free standing pen somewhere on our place and maybe an obstacle on the fence. I do practice putting the stock into the free standing pen and through various obstacles so when my dogs see that obstacle they understand the concepts. The one thing I never seem to set up is a free standing Y chute. Seems like every time one of my dogs gets into ASCA's open I find myself standing there scratching my head thinking, "I forgot to train for this."

How do you go about teaching an outrun?

I'm hesitant to answer this. I've trained so many dogs to do outruns you'd think I'd have it all figured out. However, now I have a dog without a good outrun. I think part of that is MY AGE. I'm having some problems getting where I should be.

I begin this in its tiniest form in the round pen. I start the dog at my side near the middle of the pen. I walk between the dog and the livestock doing a flank. I put enough pressure on the dog to move him out away from the stock, while he is moving away from the stock, I stop moving with him, if he is still opening up I stay in place, waiting for him to reach the top, as this happens I reward him by backing up giving him his stock. I start this early on so he will learn to move out past the stock, opening as he travels deeper behind the stock.

As training progresses, I do whatever works for my dog. I may use one or several or all of these methods. I leave my dog positioning myself out near the stock. I send my dog around; I can walk into him as he passes me to put pressure on him to move wider. Or with some dogs I will move away from the dog, taking the pressure off of them will cause them to open up on their outrun. I stand in two different locations when I do either of these techniques. Draw a straight line between the dog and the stock. Sometimes I stand to the left of the line as I send him away to me. At other times will stand to the right of the line as I send him away to me, sling-shotting him around me. Other things I may do, if shallow I stop him, calling him back to resend him. Or stop him and will not let him go until he turns out away from the stock opening up his flank.

As I said, I've trained lots of dog to do outruns. The other day I thought to myself, "I think this time I'm sending Hank to Trudy and let her get his outrun." So my youngest dog went to Trudy's for 30 days. But I couldn't live without him; I picked him when he had only been there 10 days. That is so wimpy of me.

How do you go about teaching the drive?

I start teaching the drive within the first hours of training. I expect the drive to be in place the same as the fetch and my dogs' skill at both to be moving along more or less equally. As soon as I get a nice stop I begin stopping my dogs off balance. Once they are comfortable doing that I ask for a walk up. I don't expect more than a few steps at first. Soon they will give me more. During this early stage of training I start, stop, and walk my dogs up on the stock at every point around the circle of the stock. There are four directions I work on from the beginning, clockwise – go by, counterclockwise – away to me, move into the stock – walk up, and stay facing the stock while backing away from it - back.

How do you go about teaching a stop and steady?

I begin stopping all dogs, students or my own, the first real lesson. I begin with a standing stop. It seems to me to be the simplest stop for the dog to achieve successfully and without much resistance. I put both arms out, step toward the dog and tell them to stand. 90% of the time that is exactly what I get a nice standing stop. If they don't stop I won't let them have their stock. It doesn't take long before they stop. I don't make them hold the stop for a long period of time; maybe 1/2 a second for the first couple of hours of training. As they get more practice at stopping I will lengthen the time they hold their stop.

As I am stopping the dog I am doing my part, I stop the stock too. I don't ask my dogs to stop on moving stock until they have been working for 30 to 40 hours or even more depending on the dog. I really want my dogs to trust me, putting them on a stop and letting the stock escape often makes them reluctant to stop. Dogs new to working stock aren't keen on the stock getting away. I am not going to misplace their trust by making them lose their stock during our early stages of training.

I begin the steady away from stock by introducing the word steady a second before I tell the dog to stand or down. I do this about 50 to 60 times away from stock before I apply it to the herding lesson. As the dog is moving I ask for a steady – a seconds pause – then the stop command. The pause is allowing time for the dog to slow his pace. At first I ask for a stop even if he slows, until I see he is consistently slowing in anticipation of a stop. When I see that he is approaching the stock slowly and when he is slowing on his flank, I don't stop him. All dogs are so different about this but about four to five hours I would expect to have a steady on both the walk up and the flanks.

I teach hurry as well as steady. I feel both are equally important and when teaching both it becomes apparent to the dog that they are speed related. Using both really helps to develop each one. They enhance one another especially when practiced on the flanks.

How do you handle a dog that wants to grip?

I like a dog with grip. The last thing I want to do is stop him from gripping. Gripping does need to be controlled if it is inappropriate. I've found that when a dog is 10 feet or more off his stock he cannot grip; hence gripping is not an issue. That seems like the very best way to help the dog control his grip without dampening his desire to grip. I don't want to dampen his desire to grip because biting is a dog's last line of defense. I don't want to take that last line of self-preservation away.

Often when I see my dog is going to either heel or head I encourage him. I name the grip as he gets hold. If I want heels, when he grips the heel I say "push." A nose grip I name "hit." It doesn't seem to take too long for them to catch hold of the command when it is given as they are doing it.

When do you introduce a dog to cattle?

I buy feeders in the spring; that is when the dog meets the cattle. If my dog is young, under a year, it may be across the fence or on line while I walk along with him. My dogs have from spring until October when I butcher to work cattle.

Do you work for a balance between the need for obedience to your commands and the desire to develop a thinking dog?

My dogs all have a ton of obedience on them first. Then I begin letting them think on their own more and more. When they are working on their own if they have a problem, I can help them because they have all the commands in their bag of tricks.

After I have helped them solve the problematic situation I can set it up again and again if necessary to see if they learned how to hand it. If they still need help I can help them. As with all training, practice makes perfect. As an example, the dog that has a problem going between the stock and the fence may have to practice doing that lift in hundreds of places, hundreds of times before he is confident. That is fine; it is all part of the journey.

A herding skill I like them to do on their own is move stock in a straight line. I give all my attention to the stock. If possible I stand where I can see my dog out of the corner of my eye. I pick a point; put my dog on the stock flanking until I have the stock's noses headed for that location. Then the stock's heads are right I say, "There." At first every time the stock's noses comes off that point, I give an "ah" sound which is telling my dog he is doing something wrong and needs to correct what he is doing. (This command is different than a "no" command. "No" is a correction for doing something really naughty that I don't want him to do again.) I wait a second to see if he self corrects, if not I help him by giving the flank to correct the movement of the stock. When the stock's noses are on line I once again say, "there." Remember each dog is different. One of my dogs learned the first time out. Man was born doing straight lines. The day I decided to begin this training was also the day he did it correctly after a couple, you are wrong, commands. Pert can do a straight line but it took a while for her to get the idea.

The "there" command seems to have many differing meanings. It certainly isn't one of those universal commands, same meaning for everyone. When I say, "there," it means the livestock are pointed exactly where I want them. Do what you must to keep them headed to that exact point.

If you are not familiar with this technique there is a very important issue you must remember. Do not watch the dog! His movement to the left or right doesn't tell you where the stock is going. You must watch your livestock's noses or heads. It doesn't matter where your dog moves, if the heads are pointed to the place you want them to go the dog is right. If you watch the dog, giving him the wrong information or even the right information but at the wrong time he will have an incredibly difficult time learning this skill. Also be sure to give your dog time to think about the, you're wrong, correction so he can self-correct. He needs time to process and self-correct. This is how he learns to make those drive lines on his own while you smile and keep your mouth shut.

Pens are great fun to train. First I am in the pen with my dogs, in the middle directing and helping them learn to work a pen, against the fence, slow and easy. We move from pen to pen, big, small, tiny, fenced, solid walls, every type pen I have around here and the other locations where I train. When I feel they understand working in a pen I up the ante. I move first against the fence, within hours of training I move out of the pen. I'm working on the flanking commands, the dog working the edges and at an easy walk. I introduce the inside flank with me on the other side of the fence. I begin with full circles. When he can do that I begin half and quarter flanks between the livestock and me. Before too long he knows his inside flanks.

Then we begin taking stock out of pens. I introduce the, "get around." command. That means they decide the best way to approach the take. As you know all dogs have a favorite side and that maybe how my dog decides to do all takes. Other dogs or more ambidextrous and will read the situation taking the stock out as they see necessary. In most cases it really doesn't matter. A dog that always uses his best side will become very proficient doing pen work his way. Perhaps better and safer than if I am forcing him to use his bad side. I'm not saying the dog shouldn't know how to use both flanks to do a take out of a pen. I am saying when I want them to think on their own, I say, "get around," and I don't care which way he goes, I trust him to work on his own.

Those are a few examples of how I train first then let the dog do it on its own. I prefer to train this way because I've had success using this approach. I like to have commands in my dogs' bag of trick so I can help or assist as necessary. I've outlined only a few techniques I use, I have tons I've learned from books, instructors, clinics, watching, etc. I will use one or many, every lesson and method I use it totally dependent on the dog and what works for him.

When do you know a dog is ready to trial?

That is pretty easy; when my dog demonstrates that he knows the rules regardless of where we are he is ready to go. For me the rules are he will stop, walk up, and knows his flacks, has a steady and hurry, he can fetch and at least cross drive.

I first enter my dogs in the American Herding Breed Association's (AHBA) and the American Kennel Club's (AKC) test classes, Junior Herd Dog (JHD) and Pre-Trial (PT) respectively. These pass/fail classes give me an opportunity to put miles on my dogs without a great deal of pressure. This allows me to work my dog in the trialing environment without the stress that getting a qualifying score puts on me, which of course rolls downhill to my dogs. In both organizations since these are pass/fail test classes I can run my dog as much as I like or can afford.

Usually, while certainly not always, once I have put some miles on in the test classes I begin to enter my dogs in the Australian Shepherd Club of American' s (ASCA) started. ASCA's started is actually easier than either of the two test classes mentioned above. If my dog has been doing well in the test classes I feel he can do fine in ASCA's started. I continue to run my dog in ASCA until he has earned a Working Trial Champion (WTCH).

I'm always thrilled when my dogs earn their ASCA advanced titles in sheep and cattle. That is when I can run in my favorite of all programs, Post Advanced. I love Post Advanced and the nuances of pulling the stock slightly toward me on the cross drive just enough to make a drive through the second obstacle. Very fun!

I will also begin working on titling him in AHBA, moving him along as I find time. Here in Washington my partners and I host six AHBA events a year. Because I'm a host I don't always have time to run my dogs in our trials.

When my dog has its WTCH I feel pretty confident he is ready for AKC's started classes. That is usually when I begin trialing in AKC. Sometimes I can't wait, and start running my dogs in AKC sooner. The pattern for my dogs has been they earn their WTCH first, next their AHBA Championship (HTCH) and last the AKC Championship HC.

Are you a stockdog judge? What do you look for in the "perfect" run?

I was an ASCA and an AKC judge. I've stopped judging for both of those programs because I no longer enjoy judging. I don't like it even a little bit; I'd rather help people than judge them. I am still an AHBA judge only because I put on at least six AHBA trials every year. If something unforeseen happens to a judge at the last minute I can always step in and cover it.

I wrote a couple of paragraphs then realized you are asking for the perfect run. I was talking about errors. Wrong. So this is VERY SIMPLE; the stock is kept together as they are WALKED through the prescribed course. The dog has full control. The handler, in a conversational voice, is the coach giving the commands only as needed, telling the dog when to turn the direction of the flow and at what point to move it forward again. The dog holds his line once set on it until directed to change it.

Simple huh! Don't we all wish every one of our runs happened that way?

How do you feel about trialing? Do you trial in other venues?

I love to trial and I have a very competitive nature. As I have outlined above I move my dogs from one titling program to the next as they progress in their training. Over the years I've been privileged to be the partner while one dog or another has earned most of the titles available in ASCA, AHBA and AKC. It has been fun and I'm looking forward to trialing Hank this year, 2014. Hopefully we will complete his working or herding championship in all three programs. I think the journey with him will be very fun, it has been so far.

The one herding program I have not run my Aussies in is United States Border Collie Handers' Association (USBCHA) although I have run our Border Collie in that venue. I feel I should do that with my Aussies. In this area we have several Aussies doing very well. One handsome Aussie, a Mr. Man son named Dan, owned by Billie Richardson of Canada, qualified for the USBCHA Nursery finals in 2013 and placed 26th overall. I am proud of dog and owner. Debbi Dunne of Oregon, with her dog Spyder, has won a challenging Pro/Novice class. Trudy Viklund, (one of the contributing trainers for this book, and someone I deeply respect) has been running her Mr. Man daughter Tic in Pro/Novice over the years. She is now running a Tic son. We have more people with nice Aussies of various working breeding showing interest running their dogs in Novice/Novice and Ranch. Good for them. I need to get off my lazy rear end and get out there too.

What is the most important tip you would like to give someone interested in training an Aussie for stock work?

Relax and enjoy the journey.

TRUDY VIKLUND

Trudy and her husband run a sheep farm in Molalla, OR. In recent years they have done leased ground grazing and custom grazing of cattle and sheep. Currently they grow Christmas trees, train working dogs and raise lambs for market and private sale. They try to raise their stock in as natural environment as possible, and most work is done on pasture. They do pasture lambing and use guardian dogs as predator control. The dogs are used to sort, treat, move, load and transport the stock.

Trudy's interest in dogs began when she was young, training dogs in obedience and agility. Trudy has trained a variety of dogs, including Corgis, Beardies, Shelties, Collies, Border Collies, Kelpies, Rotties and of course, Australian Shepherds. Trudy emphasizes teaching the dog and handler to work as a team, with the goal of calm, quiet, confident control of livestock. Her focus is on allowing (and helping) the dog to properly feel balance, take control of the stock, and carefully manage movement.

She enjoys trialing in ASCA, AKC, AHBA, USBCHA, and cowdog trials with her own Aussies, as well as handling dogs for clients. She has trialed and/or handled several dogs to Working Trial Championships (ASCA), AKC Championships and AHBA Championships. She is currently competing with her Aussies: Newt in Pro-Novice and Jill in Nursery class in USBCHA, and as well as AKC, AHBA, and ASCA trials.

To contact Trudy:

trudy@doublevstockdogs.com

www.DoubleVstockdogs.com

How long have you been involved in training and trialing Aussies? How did that involvement come about?

As a kid I groomed, trained and showed Akitas for a conformation kennel and I did agility/obedience with my Labrador. One of my neighbors had an Aussie, and they asked me to train him for them. I taught him obedience and agility and did 4H competitions with him. I was also involved with showing horses, and Aussies were common to see around the horse shows.

Training my neighbor's dog and seeing Aussies at the horse shows made me really love Australian Shepherds. I also loved my Akitas and Labrador, but I planned that someday I would get an Aussie so I could learn about herding dogs.

I got my first Aussie just before I married Dave. Dave and I were fresh out of school, and didn't have much to our names, but we knew we wanted to run our own stock on our own place. He had a little Border Collie, and I wanted an Aussie. I got her from a breeder near the Oregon coast. Her name was Kes, and she was a great dog.

At the time, I was working on Warmblood Horse Ranch and I trained Kes on the geese that had gone feral on the ranch. The geese would see us coming and break for the pond, so she had to learn to cover quickly and balance to hold them, otherwise training was over that day. After we did about as much training as we could on our own, and on nasty, rogue geese, I went looking for help. I started attending clinics and training her on sheep and cattle, and when we were ready, I started trialing her.

Where did you get your first Aussie? How did you first hear about the breed?

See Above

What makes the Aussie different from other dogs that work stock?

The Aussie is special because it originated in the United States. Australian Shepherd is the working dog many people associated with the American cowboy and the Basque shepherds. Aussies were used by sheep and cattle ranchers on the open range in the West. Similar to American culture, the Aussie is a melting pot of different herding breeds. Major sheep producing areas in the world have breeds that are used to work the large flocks and to help the ranchers in those areas. Some commonly known ones are the Border Collie from the Scotland/England area and Kelpies from Australia. Each breed is well suited to its environment, terrain, and handling style of the ranchers. The Aussie is the American version of this all purpose ranch dog, suited to the varied climates/terrain/livestock found in the US. There are also breeds developed primarily for cattle, like the Heeler, Hangin Tree Cow dogs, and Catahoulas. My favorite dog is sensible and strong enough to work range sheep, but gritty and forward enough for cattle, and that is the intended purpose of the Aussie.

Another defining characteristic of the breed is the way its registries work. Some working breeds have separate registries for the conformation and working variations, causing a defined divide in those breeds. U.S. Aussie breeders typically use AKC and/or ASCA registry for both. Because of its melting pot heritage, different styles of livestock handling by breeders and the way the registries keep the dogs united, it leaves the variation and diversity in types of Aussies that can be found today.

Is it the Aussie temperament or looks that makes the Aussie special?

Not all Aussies look alike and not all Aussies have the same temperament. That is what makes the Aussie special. There is strength in a breed that can maintain diversity and is essential to keeping a breed strong in its working ability. It could maybe be the heart of the Aussie that makes them most special. They will give you their heart, everything they have, if you ask it. It is the heart of the Aussie that I love most.

What do you look for in a puppy? What do you consider the ideal pup?

I believe the parents are the most important aspects when choosing an ideal puppy. Working dogs are difficult to breed and select as pups because you often times can't see the traits you are selecting for in young puppy. When choosing for physical traits, you have predictors to look at in young puppies. Working traits often times can't be seen until they are older, and then it can be difficult to distinguish from environmental factors. Consequently, I like to judge a litter on the parents.

To me, balance is probably the single most important inherited trait. Most of my training and natural work I want from my dogs stems from their balance. A dog with strong balance is likely to make the right decisions when left to work independently. A lack of balance is easily passed on. The less natural balance in a dog, the more mechanical its work will tend to be once trained. To keep my dogs natural and independent in their work, I like to keep strong balance in them genetically. I watch how the parents approach the stock. I want them to be confident and direct, with a low head and tail set. I want them to approach directly, with a calm manner. Can they maintain balance, do they hold the stock while flanking?

I like the parents to be willing and confident to break as they flank, and desire to turn in and hold pressure. I want the parents to be able to move quickly laterally into a position of pressure, and then steady enough to hold that position. I want them comfortable enough to come forward and create motion from a position of balance, without the need to rush, bark or slice. These traits are all important to a dog's ability to balance, so these are the things I will look for in the pedigree of my litter.

My ideal pup would come from a litter with parents whom are most likely to throw those traits into the pups. From that litter I would choose the pup whom I felt drawn too. I do not think there is always a best and least pup in a litter, I feel all the pups in a litter can be great if they are paired with a person who believes in them. I prefer a calm pup, who is steady and confident, and a sweet pup, whom would like to bond to me.

What do you consider the ideal age for starting a pup on stock? Do you start on sheep? Do you ever use any other stock, like ducks or goats, to start your pups?

I do not think there is a set ideal age for all dogs. I do think it is best that dogs do not have a lot of training stress on them to control livestock when they are too young. If dogs are not confident to take control they will slice and move stock with their body motion, puppies will do this anyway, just playing with the stock.

One of my litters of pups, I was able to train 5 of the puppies myself. Two of the puppies I excitedly started working them at 6 months. One puppy, I started at 9 months, and the last 2 pups I started when they were 11 months. All the pups were raised in different, but somewhat comparable homes. It was a good lesson for me. I watched the two pups started at 11 months flourish in the training. They caught up and surpassed the ones I started early, within a couple months. They were mentally mature enough to handle the pressures of controlling stock properly and did not practice a lot of puppy behaviors that I had to train out of them. The ones I started young did train up nicely, and all the pups ended up as equally good stock dogs, but it did show me that there was not much benefit to starting them really young. I found that, for me, waiting works well and is maybe less stress overall.

Since then, I typically expose my pups to stock at random intervals as they are growing up. I encourage the pups to balance to me, but no pressure to do so. I prefer to wait until they are close to a year before starting to really train on them. If a dog seemed immature at a year, I would wait a month and then try again, until the dog seemed ready. I think when they are getting close to year they have developed a better relationship with me, compared to when they are still quite young.

I have started all my dogs on sheep. I like calm sheep that flock well and do not tend to panic or run for starting a pup, sheep that are slower and allow the pup to feel a flight zone. I haven't used anything else, as our cows often had calves with them, which might be dangerous for a pup.

How do you raise your Aussies? Are they house dogs or kennel dogs?

I try to raise my dogs to be as well adjusted and confident as possible. When I am raising a puppy I put a lot of time and effort into building a good relationship with that puppy. I want the puppy to trust and respect me, and to love me and look to me for guidance. I take them to lots of places and let them have lots of different experiences. I set the puppy up to make both right and wrong decisions and learn from them.

My dogs are house dogs, but they are also comfortable kenneled. I travel a lot for work and my dogs travel with me most places. When traveling, there are some places where they will have to be kenneled while I work, so I make sure they are used to it. At home my dogs may be kenneled if I am working or doing a project that is unsafe for them to be around. Or if my bitch is in season, either her or my dog would be kenneled. Otherwise they are inside or outside with me.

When in training, if a young dog is dealing with intense lessons, I like to kennel the young dog approximately an hour before and after those lessons so the dog can process the learning better.

How important is the relationship between an Aussie and its person?

The handler/dog relationship is the most important thing for a stock dog. The dog must trust and respect the handler, and the handler must believe in the dog and have respect for the work the dog is doing. Any rift in the relationship, will surface in a working environment. In many ways, the dog will learn to handle the stock in the same way the dog is handled by the handler. A quiet, calm handler will have the respect of the dog and the dog will learn to handle the stock quietly and with respect.

A good relationship between dog and handler can overcome weakness in either partner. When the relationship is not good, any weakness in either partner will be enhanced. Sometimes it is not the best, or most talented dog, nor the most experienced handler, that can do the best work. Sometimes a lesser pair with a good relationship can get the best results. A good relationship between dog and handler will strengthen both partners. Only when a team has a strong relationship can they reach their full potential.

Do you let your pups follow you around when you are doing chores?

Sure, I like to let my pup hang with me while I do chores, as long as I feel it is a good experience for the pup. Lots of times our only regular daily chore is to drive out and feed the guardian dogs, and drive through and check the stock. A few months in the winter we supplement feed out on the pasture daily. When we do this, a pup can ride out and learn to stay on the vehicle while feeding and watch the stock move about. I like this because it encourages the pup to exhibit self control, watch the stock calmly, and keeps the pup safe. I wouldn't let a pup run fences or rush stock while I was doing chores, and I prefer an older pup not learn to be to overly complacent around stock.

When do you like a pup to show interest in stock? Does it matter? Is there an age where you would start to worry if you hadn't seen any interest yet?

Mine typically show interest fairly young, but they are not ready for real training pressures yet. I think it is convenient for a pup to start showing interest later, only because it makes my life easier before they are ready for training. Really, as long as they have an interest when I am ready to start the training, I think either is fine. I think it is important to not start training until the pup is fast enough to head without slicing, and not until the pup is mature enough to handle the pressures of taking control directly. Different dogs mature at different rates, but my last several dogs I started at around 1 year of age. Mine have always had an interest in stock by 1 yr, if one didn't and I liked the dog, I would be patient and give it more time.

Is there an age when an Aussie is too old to start on stock?

That would probably depend on what are the expectations you have of the dog when it is finished. To start an elderly dog to stock, the dog may never reach its full potential, but it may make a fine dog for what is needed. A young healthy adult dog that is talented can be started late and still be a great dog. Maybe to start them when they are in the peak of their learning ages would be ideal for the ultimate success and ease of training.

What sort of stock do you use in the beginning? How many?

We raise sheep and always have sheep, so that is what we use for starting our dogs. Some years we have had cattle, but in recent years, we haven't. The number would depend on the temperament of the sheep available and on what I was trying to develop in the dog at the time. If I was trying to tighten a dog up, I may use a smaller group, and if I am trying to free the dog up I would use a larger group. The dog needs to have experience with both, so I would do both and then focus on which the dog needed the most work with. I like to start a dog on calm sheep who are not inclined to run, I like the dog to be able to feel the flight zone of the sheep and be able to apply pressure to it. In other words, I prefer not overly dull, nor overly reactive sheep. That is more important to me than the number of sheep.

Do you use a round pen? If so, at what point in training?

I don't have a round pen at my farm, but I have done some training in round pens. One of the farms I train at has a round pen, and I do use it with some dogs. I use it when I think the dog may try to push the stock away from the handler, or if I think the dog might try to go off contact. Lots of dogs I have trained without ever using a round pen, and some dogs I have done a fair bit in the round pen with them. Most of my own dogs do not do a lot in a round pen, just enough that they are comfortable with it, and then move on.

Do you ever use an older dog to help with training? If so, in what way and for how long?

I will use a trained dog if the dog being trained was unable to handle a situation on its own. If I were to work a young dog in an area that they may not be able to handle all situations I might bring a trained dog as back up, to hold sheep within an area, or to retrieve the sheep if they have gone too far for the young dog. If I am asking a young dog to hold a large group off feed, at first I may have an older dog to help assist. A large group being held off may try to curl around a young dog while it is distracted holding one specific area. The young dog may not have the experience to know when/how to release and reposition at the right time to hold back all areas. An older dog can help with this. The older dog is typically asked to stay off the stock and used minimally, so the young dog is handling most of the situation on its own.

What do you like pups/dogs to know before you introduce them to stock? Do you teach any commands off stock?

If I am only putting a pup on stock in a controlled environment to give it exposure, or to satisfy my curiosity as to what the pup may do, I will often times have very little, to no commands on the pup.

Prior to actually starting one of my dogs, I like for them to have developed a good relationship with me off stock. I want the dog to trust me and be respectful, and I want the dog to have learned what a correction is. I want my corrections to mean I don't like a behavior, and for the dog to change or try something different. I do not want them to be worried or fearful of a correction, nor do I want them to ignore a correction. I don't want to be using a lot of commands when they are first on stock, so I really don't focus on training a lot of commands. I prefer the dog to understand pressure, approval and disapproval and utilize that, so the dog is learning principles and not listening for commands.

I try to teach my pups to make decisions, to be somewhat independent but also to look to me for guidance when needed. The main things they will learn as young dogs are typically to come to me, to respect a boundary and to stay when told. Usually they have learned to sit or lie down at some point also. Often I will teach a dog to walk behind me when asked, but I don't do a lot of that, so the dog is comfortable to move freely around me also. I also don't expect these things to be perfect when first put on stock. I will teach stops, walk up and flank commands only on stock, as those commands are flight zone dependent.

More important than teaching my young dogs specific commands, might be to teach them self control. My young dogs can have a tendency towards impulsiveness and nothing will bring out impulsiveness like herding livestock. In order to help prepare them for this, I work with them as they grow, to develop self control. Each dog may have different things that will elicit them to have a lack of self-control, so I will tailor it to suit the individual. A dog may be impulsive about seeing other dogs run, or running through a gate, or to chase rabbits, whatever it is for each dog, I will use opportunities to help the young dog develop self-control.

Do you ever use any tools when training, like a long line or a stock stick?

I have used stocks sticks, plastic bags, rolled up bags of feed, a coil of rope, a hat, really anything handy that might help a dog to understand a cue. Stock stick is my most common one. I have occasionally used long lines when necessary to help people train their dogs in certain circumstances. When I train my own dogs, I typically don't have much use for a long line when working stock.

What do you like to see in an Aussie in its first few sessions on stock? What would tell you that it is a good prospect?

I love to see a pup who tries to control the stock and has a confident manner. I hope the pup will work the heads and show some feel for balance and the flight zone. I prefer a quiet pup, who doesn't bark, and one that shows good focus and intensity. If a pup shows ability to hold or apply pressure properly at a young age, that is always exciting to see.

Can you describe the best pup you ever started? What made it special and where is it today?

Hard to say, I have been lucky to start a lot of really nice dogs. Different dogs have been the best at different things. Tick was the best dog I have had at holding pressure, Newt has been my best outrunner. Lots of pups I have trained, have been good a different things. I could see these traits in those dogs early on as I started them. Those traits were in those dogs and I only had to develop or support them. Every breeding I do, I think my dogs get better and I also have more experience at starting dogs, which helps a lot.

My most recent dog is maybe my best all around so far. Jillaroo has been great to start. She feels balance nicely, has nice amount of eye and flanks along the flight zone well. She is forward and confident, and a good listener. Right now she is working on our farm and I am being serious about her training, taking her to different locations and working different stock, pushing her to see what she is ready for. She is doing better and more consistent work than any of my other dogs have done at a comparable age. She is the product of me understanding more about how to breed and start my dogs, so I am really excited about her.

Tell us a little about your training style. How often do you work a started dog? What skills do you like to train first? When do you move on to the next skill?

My training style probably revolves most around balance of the livestock. I feel if the dog truly understands how to balance the stock, all training can stem from there. Proper control, distance, speed, rate, shape, stops, holding, forcing, driving, fetching, outruns, really everything can be taught as a form or piece of balance. A dog will need to learn how to balance different types and numbers of livestock, the smaller the number of stock, the more defined the balance point will be, a larger groups of stock will have a broader balance point. Also they need to learn to balance to different points and pressures, balance towards the handler, towards an arbitrary point, against a draw, into a draw, along side of a draw, etc. If the dog is using proper balance, then the dog understands the principles of herding and will be able to work any type of livestock, in any type of area and at any distance. As I train my dogs, I will teach them something new, but always go back to a simple form of balance, to test them that they understand that all lessons pertain to balance in some way.

Once I decide a dog is ready for serious training I will train them often and will move along fairly quickly in the training. If the dog is training well, I will work it nearly every day, with occasional days off. If the dog gets to a point where it isn't learning as well, I will give it some time off to mature.

I do have a basic order of training that I follow, but it is not written in stone and I will change it up based on the dogs needs and the situations available. As a dog gets an idea of new concept, I move on to the next, but always go back and review old concepts. Any hole that shows up in the review and I will go back to that area of training for a bit, and then move forward again. When I train, any error or misunderstanding the dog might have, I stop, and try to set up the situation again, and have the dog do it again, properly. For example, if I have already taught a dog about proper shapes of a flank, and the dogs gives me a slicing or rushy flank, I will stop the dog, put it back in the original position and make it re-do the flank. However, if I am working on a difficult concept and the dog gets the concept, but did do a slicey flank, I might forgive the poor flank in the interest of the dog getting the new, more difficult concept. I would go back and work on fixing the flank later. This is where experience in training is important, deciding when to give back to the dog and when to ask the dog for more.

How do you go about teaching an outrun?

First, I teach, or encourage, the dog to seek the balance point. Then I teach the dog that it must follow the flight zone (or flank properly) to get to the balance point. The dog is taught how to (or expected to) feel for the flight zone as it is approaching from the outside of the flight zone. I make a great effort to get my dogs experience on stock with varying flight zones and on fields of various terrain, so the dog is confident to do this regardless of the terrain, obstacles or type of livestock.

I teach the dog to cast using a triangular pattern between myself, the dog and the stock. I do not allow the dog to cross to my side of the triangle. The more obtuse the angle between myself and the dog, the more difficult it is for the dog to break out. I start at an acute angle and increase difficulty by slowly moving to a more and more obtuse angle. I do this to encourage the dog to run wider as it gets further away from me and to teach the dog to be bending off the stock, and not my presence. When you are able to caste your dog from an obtuse angle, it is in essence the same as doing a redirect. Once I have a reliable redirect, I can help a dog to fix an outrun from almost any position.

How do you go about teaching the drive?

I want the dog to think a drive is not so different from a fetch. I want the dog to still use its balance to work a drive. When I teach a dog to drive I try to show them that they are still balancing. Only difference in driving is they are balancing to an arbitrary point, instead of to me. I need to communicate that point to them, and make them understand they are to cover any deviation from that line. I will use pushing away from draws, guarding draws, releasing into draws, working lines and holding pressure to help a dog to understand this. I want them to be pushing and controlling the heads while driving, not just following and pressing stock forward. This makes the difference between a dog who can only create motion and a dog who can both create and control motion. If the dog has learned to do this properly from behind on a fetch, they will transfer it to driving pretty easily. To learn to do this properly on a fetch the dog needs experience in fetching stock that do not want to fetch. I prefer my dogs to be able to fetch non-fetchy stock before teaching a drive.

How do you go about teaching a stop and steady?

Typically I start teaching a stop by trying to figure out what will bring the dog to a natural stop. I would consider a natural stop to be when the dog stopped on its own, because it felt right to the dog and the dog was in a position of control. Some dogs will do a natural stop on balance, some will if you go up to a fence line, or a corner. Some dogs you will need to block them a few times to encourage them to stop. I prefer to have the dog stop with the stock in front of them, not me, if possible.
Once the dog stops, I will release pressure by stepping back, and allowing the dog to move into the stock with whatever feels comfortable to the dog. I do not pressure the dog at that point to do a specific move, whatever feels right to the dog because it is the release, or reward, for the stop. I practice bringing the dog to a natural stop several times until it becomes easy for the dog, then I will start to put a word to it. I want the dog to associate the stop with control of the stock and then a release of pressure. Even if I have an obedience command on the dog that would stop it, I will still do this method with the dog so it learning to respond to pressure and the situation, not an obedience command at first.

To teach a dog to steady, I would use a similar method, it is just in motion. I use a steady command to slow a dog down on a walk up. To other people it may mean something different, I use a steady command to either end a flank with a walk up, or to slow down an already existing walk up. My steady is associated with coming into the stock. I wait on teaching a steady command until the dog is holding balance fairly well. I will make sure the dog will do a natural steady to hold balance before adding a command to it. As the dog is fetching stock to me I will walk backwards as the stock are coming, and indicate to the dog I need it to steady. I may pressure the stock so they cannot pass me, and I will not allow the dog to flank out of the pressure, nor will I allow it to burst the pressure by coming into the flight zone. If the stock slow down, as I do not allow the stock to pass me, and I do not allow the dog to flank or press in to avoid the pressure, then the dog's only option to maintain balance, and control, is to be steady. I continue walking back and releasing the pressure so the dog knows it is still to come forward and be applying pressure on a steady, not just let go. I only ask a young dog to maintain this for short segments at first, until the dog is able to handle the pressure longer.

As long as a dog is flanking appropriately, I do not teach a dog a slowing command on a flank. I would correct a dog for inappropriate flanking in general, but I do not teach dog a specific command to slow its flanks. If I give a short flank, I would expect the dog to take the flank with the appropriate speed.

How do you handle a dog that wants to grip?

There are different reasons a dog may grip. Some dogs may grip when they get out of position and don't know how to fix it, for that type of dog I would help it maintain position or teach it get back to a correct position when it is wrong. Many dogs may grip under pressure. Those dogs I would put in pressure situations and work with them on how to handle the different scenarios calmly. Lots of dogs will grip when to close if they are nervous, those dogs need time and experience to be confident and comfortable under pressure when close to livestock. If a dog is gripping a lot, I try to observe the situations and determine the causes. I don't want to make the dog think a grip is always bad, I want the dog to learn to try other tools first, and to still have a grip if needed. When working through these scenarios, I try to correct the dog for the action that led to the grip (like getting out of position) and not necessarily for the grip itself.

When do you introduce a dog to cattle?

This would depend on what cattle were available and the temperament of the dog. Cattle can hurt a dog, and I think it is really important that the dog have a good experience in its first couple exposures to cattle. I like a dog to have a reliable stop, a call off, and I would want to know that for the most part the dog will feel/respect the flight zone. Once I had those, I would feel good about introducing my dog to cattle. I want those things so I can keep the dog and cattle safe when training. The tamer the cattle, the more relaxed might be on those requirements, the more difficult the cattle the more strict I would be that the dog had them.

Do you work for a balance between the need for obedience to your commands and the desire to

develop a thinking dog?

Of course, you need to have both. If you do not practice both it is easy to become unbalanced. Ideally, if your partnership with the dog is good, your commands will match the dog's instincts. It is simple to keep this balance, if you are aware of it. I want my dogs to be obedient to me. If I make the effort to say a command, I want my dog to obey it. If I do not say anything, I would expect my dog to cover, hold or balance the stock as they saw right for the situation. If the dog is not understanding what my intention is, it is my job as the handler to be sure the dog understand the intention, it is the dogs job to carry it out. With an advanced dog I would expect the dog to be able to handle me changing my intention multiple times in a row, thus taking multiple commands quickly, and adjusting the balance point each time. However, a younger dog I wouldn't expect as much. You can have both in a dog, and both are necessary for the dog to reach its full potential.

When doing a new or unfamiliar task with a dog, I would expect to have to do more communication to let the dog know what the expectation is. If it was a familiar task and the dog knew what the goal was I would expect not say much. As an example, in a trial, I expect dogs to be receiving commands, since most dogs would have no way of knowing what the course was. My dogs trial on different courses, and I typically do not practice course work with my dogs. As a result, in a trial, my dog has only me to rely on for information as to what the course is. However, when sending a trained dog to gather a field or drive a familiar route, I would expect the dog to know the task and carry it out. The two are very different, and I like my dogs to be able to do both.

When do you know a dog is ready to trial?

That would very much depend on what type of trial you are planning to go to. As a base rule I want my dogs able to control any temperament of stock that I am likely to encounter at the trial. I wouldn't want to enter my dog and find that the stock were over my dog's head in ability to control. I would want to know I could stop my dog at any point in the trial I needed to, and that I could send my dog to any position needed for the intended course. I would want my dog working at home to a higher standard than what is required for the trial level I am entering. I would not to be stretching my dogs abilities in a trial. The dog should be comfortable and confident with the requirements of the course entered.

Are you a stockdog judge? What do you look for in the "perfect" run?

I have judged trials and I like to see a dog who is really working to communicate intention to the livestock. I like to see teamwork between dog and handler, the handler giving subtle commands when needed, so the dog knows what the job is. I like the dog to be confident and direct in its method of control. I like to see the stock relaxed and moving smoothly through the course and at pace just slightly quicker than what the stock would choose on their own. The straighter and the steadier the stock move, the more control I feel the dog has.

How do you feel about trialing? Do you trial in other venues?

I very much enjoy trialing. I enjoy testing our progress in a difficult environment. I like to watch my dog handle unfamiliar stock, in an unfamiliar environment and to see where our relationship is when put to the test. It can show me where any holes in my training are, as many things can go unnoticed at home, on familiar stock and territory. Watching other dogs and handlers work through trial situations gives me ideas on what I want in my own dogs and also what is achievable. There is a lot of variation in difficulty of livestock and difficulty of courses in various trials, even within a venue. I enjoy preparing for harder and harder trials and pushing myself and my dog to be ready for more challenge. Trialing also encourages me to strive for perfection in my stock work at home. This results in me, and my dog, handling our own stock quieter and with less stress. I have trialed in every venue in my general area and I have enjoyed different aspects in all the venues. My favorite venues are the ones that really stretch a dog and handler in abilities and the ones that judge on how the stock move through the course. The reason I like to be judged on how the stock are moved is because, to me, that is the challenge, for my dog and I figure out and display the best way to move the livestock through the intended course. I believe the livestock are the best judge of the dog and handler.

What is the most important tip you would like to give someone interested in training an Aussie for stock work?

Believe in your dog, be willing to work hard and stay open minded. Set high goals and be willing to stretch yourself and your dogs to reach them.

MARTI PARISH

Marti Parrish has been breeding and working Australian Shepherds since the mid 1970s. She judges ASCA, AKC, CKC, and AHBA stockdog trials. Throughout the years Marti has qualified and competed in The ASCA National Finals with five of her dogs, winning the prestigious title of 1999 ASCA Champion Sheep Dog with her Justus N Katie McCain. Other notable wins include High In Trial Sheep and High in Trial at the 1985 ASCA National and 1996 National Most Promising Aussie. She has taken ten Australian Shepherds to their Working Trial Championship. She has also titled dogs at the advanced levels in AKC, CKC, and AHBA. Marti has been sharing her positive training methods with students at her farm in Washington state and at clinics conducted throughout the US and Europe. Marti is owner of the Hall of Fame Kennel "Justus", breeder of 26 Working Trial Champions and 13 Hall of Fame sires and dams.

To contact Marti:

425-334-6272

justusaussie@earthlink.net

Where did you get your first Aussie? How did you first hear about the breed?
How long have you been involved in training and trialing Aussies? How did that involvement come about?

In the early '70s I trained horses in the Carolinas. Australian Shepherds started showing up there and a lot of people who had quarter horses were getting Aussies. I was given a puppy for helping whelp a litter when the owner could not be there. That was in 1975. I called her Buff, her registered name was Parrish's Possum. She was by Jimmy Osborne's Blue Boy and out of Tony Talent's My Mistic Witch. She was registered with the National Stockdog Registry located in Butler, Indiana. Buff is the foundation of my Justus Aussies.

In 1977 I moved to Washington State and that's when I learned about ASCA and became involved in trialing. There was a lot of Aussie activity happening on the west coast.

The first stockdog trial I competed at was in the summer of 1981. That fall I went to my first ASCA National with both Buff and her daughter LuLu. It was held in Riverside, California. On the way we entered trials in Hollister, California and the Paso Robles - Templeton area, then on to the Nationals at Riverside. It was my first large dog event, the dogs did great, it was a blast and I was hooked.

What makes the Aussie different from other dogs that work stock?

I like their ability to turn on and off. When you need something done they are right there ready to help. But they can relax and just hang out with you. They don't have to be constantly entertained by you or the stock.

Is it the Aussie temperament or looks that makes the Aussie special?

It is the Aussie package that makes them special. The Aussie is a beautiful, athletic dog, with super intelligence and instinct. It is a dog who is very loyal to its master and family.

What do you look for in a puppy? What do you consider the ideal pup?

I like a bold outgoing pup that enjoys interacting with me. I make a point of showing my stockdogs in the breed ring. So i look for good structure also.

What do you consider the ideal age for starting a pup on stock? Do you start on sheep? Do you ever use any other stock, like ducks or goats, to start your pups? When do you introduce a dog to cattle?

I will let the pup on stock around 6 months of age, in a well controlled situation, on dog broke sheep, for just a few minutes, because I cannot stand the anticipation of waiting to see what they will do. Over the years I've learned to take time in starting pups. They need to be both mentally and physically mature before starting actual training. This is usually somewhere close to a year. At this point they will be able to take the corrections that are necessary in training.
I had goats here for a short time. They were fun and I loved their personalities. The goats were good for starting dogs; all the dogs were fascinated by them. But I found the goats drew the dogs in, rather than learning to give distance. So I could only use them for a few sessions with a young dog.

I introduce dogs to ducks and cattle only after they have self control on sheep, with an understanding of out, steady, and there.

How do you raise your Aussies? Are they house dogs or kennel dogs?

My dogs live in kennels and the house. Puppies do a lot of kitchen training, that's where the treats are. They learn basic manners and how to get along in the pack.

How important is the relationship between an Aussie and its person?

An Aussie wants to work for its person. So if there is a good relationship with a handler who is in charge, with good communication and respect off of stock, stock work becomes much easier.

Do you let your pups follow you around when you are doing chores?

Sometimes

When do you like a pup to show interest in stock? Does it matter? Is there an age where you would start to worry if you hadn't seen any interest yet?

I like to see interest, noticing and watching stock, when a pup is two to three months.

We always worry when we don't see immediate interest, it is our nature. We want the satisfaction of knowing our dog is perfect. But different dogs turn on at different times and in different situations. Some need repeated exposures, sometimes to different types of stock.

I had a little blue female, Molly, who I thought was a dud, really cute, but not wanting to get in there and do much with the stock. I kept persisting, taking her back to sheep every few weeks. She was over two when one day it just clicked; she went around her sheep into a pretty little fetch and never hesitated again. She went on to win High in Trial at the 1985 ASCA Nationals.

Is there an age when an Aussie is too old to start on stock?

Only if it were possible it could get hurt. I personally don't see a need to start an older dog but everyone's situation is different.

What sort of stock do you use in the beginning? How many?

I use sheep for starting dogs. Round pen work is done with three to five head. Once the dog is giving nicely to pressure we get out of the round pen and into the open and at times work on larger groups.

Do you use a round pen? If so, at what point in training?

My round pen is about 75 feet in diameter. I use it for starting dogs to keep a controlled situation. I also will use it occasionally throughout training if I need a tighter area, pulling off fences, pen work etc.

Do you ever use an older dog to help with training? If so, in what way and for how long?

Only on a large group of cattle if I need to help build confidence in a young dog.

What do you like pups/dogs to know before you introduce them to stock? Do you teach any commands off stock?

I like to have a sit or down and a good recall. I like the dog responding to me with good manners, a dog willing to listen to me. I teach directional commands on the stock.

Do you ever use any tools when training, like a long line or a stock stick?

I use long 6 to 8 foot light bamboo poles. I grow my own bamboo.

What do you like to see in an Aussie in its first few sessions on stock? What would tell you that it is a good prospect?

I like a dog willing to go around its stock, seeing the whole group.

Can you describe the best pup you ever started? What made it special and where is it today?

Fortunately I've had a lot of "best" pups. The easiest pup I ever started was Sioux. She just naturally fell into a fetch right to begin with, reading and rating her stock. When Sioux was only about 5 months old, Krista Dunlap, then 10 years old, took her to the Skagit County Fairgrounds and did duck demos. The two youngsters put on quite a show.

She grew up to be WTCH Justus Sioux RD. She competed successfully in the 1990 Regional Futurity, the 1993 ASCA Finals, and Won High in Trial Sheep at the 1993 Nationals Pre Trial.

Tell us a little about your training style. How often do you work a started dog? What skills do you like to train first? When do you move on to the next skill?

I develop the fetch first, getting the dog to give to pressure on their corners and squaring up. Letting the dog stay on their feet, control the heads and getting them to give distance. This is the major fault I see when traveling around to judge. Folks are letting their young dogs work way too close and tight.
Once the dogs are out, we can work on hitting balance and training "there" ... turning into and walking up on their stock. The fetch is the time to start training this all important word that you will use, again and again, in your advanced training.
I start small out runs at this point also. Setting the stock, handler, and dog so you get the desired outcome, gradually expanding distances.

I like to work my young dogs three or so times a week. I'm usually not in a hurry with them now.

How do you go about teaching the drive?

The drive comes when your "steering wheel" is in place. Once you can pull your dog off the top, out of balance, around the stock and you, in either direction. Stopping the dog in a position to move the stock off the handler into a parallel drive to begin, gradually working this exercise until the dog can cross in front of the handler moving the stock away from the handler. It is important for the dog to learn to drive in the open and not just up a fence. Driving is against most dogs instinct so you need to be patient, accept and reward small successes.

How do you go about teaching a stop and steady?

These come during the fetch training. Most dogs when kicked out off their stock will eventually find balance. This is a spot where they are comfortable to walk on straight, "there", to the stock and bring them to the handler. This is the spot where you can ask a young dog to down and they will be comfortable in doing so. I don't ever ask for a down from a young dog until well into a session when they have had time to blow off some steam and only in a position that will not cause the dog to loose their stock. Set your dog up for success. This is where I also begin to train the steady. Using a calming voice, pressure from the stick or my hands, and slowing my pace, asking the dog to steady and slow it's pace.

How do you handle a dog that wants to grip?

Depends upon the individual dog and how much pressure they can take and what kind of grip.

Do you work for a balance between the need for obedience to your commands and the desire to develop a thinking dog?

I start a dog with very few commands. They learn to give to the pressure of my body, my stick, and "out". They hear and learn "there" and "steady". All the time being allowed to stay on their feet, think, watch the heads and control their stock. A dog that is started this way, being allowed to work, is more willing to be obedient when the time comes to do more precision work.

When do you know a dog is ready to trial?

When the handler feels comfortable with it. When the dog is staying off and controlling its livestock nicely. And the dog is working with the handler rather than on its own agenda.

I personally like my own dogs to have a good understanding of driving, a nice wide outrun, and flanking commands, so they are pretty much ready to move up the levels.

Are you a stockdog judge? What do you look for in the "perfect" run?

Yes I judge ASCA, AKC, AHBA, and CKC.

I like to see a dog quietly and calmly controlling its livestock around the course with a minimum of commands from the handler.

How do you feel about trialing? Do you trial in other venues?

I love trialing. I love taking the training that I have done with my dog and applying it to the precision of the stockdog courses.

I've finished ten WTCH dogs and put Advanced titles on dogs in AKC, AHBA, and CKC.

What is the most important tip you would like to give someone interested in training an Aussie for stock work?

"Set your dog up for success."

Get your dog to give to pressure. Aussies are pushy and need to learn to give to pressure right from the beginning.

Do your homework and train your dogs. Give your dog the opportunity to learn to control the livestock. Gather as much information from as many different sources as you can. Go to clinics, take lessons, read. Then use the knowledge that works for you. The main thing is mileage. If you are having problems, get some help from someone with experience. If you are not ready to trial go anyways, watch the runs and ask questions. You can learn a lot by just watching the dogs work.

DANA MACKENZIE

Dana Mackenzie has been involved with Australian Shepherds since first observing Aussies at a stock trial in 1985. She has trained more than 25 Working Trial Champions in ASCA and has been judging in ASCA for almost a decade. She also judges for AKC, AHBA and CKC and championed many dogs in AHBA. Dana lives in North Texas and travels extensively throughout the year to judge, trial and give clinics.

"Herding dogs have been my constant companions for the past 30 years. Our jobs have ranged from the "cowboy" life on a 11,000 acre ranch, to looking after sheep and goats at my present location in north central Texas.

As I have gotten "longer in the tooth" my dogs have progressed from helping occasionally to doing 95% of my work. I can't even imagine life without a furry head or cold nose bumping my hand. I certainly could never have lived the kind of life I have lived and now live without my working buddies!

Somewhere along the road dog training, trialing and judging came in.

Looking back now, I wouldn't change a thing. The outdoor life has suited me well. It has been an honor to have known, loved and worked with exceptional dogs and certainly, a lifelong pleasure meeting the stock dog folks I have encountered along the way."

To contact Dana:

Danamack@brazosnet.com

How long have you been involved in training and trialing Aussies? How did that involvement come about?

I have had Aussies since around '84-'85. I was working on an 11,000 acre brushy ranch taking care of either 600 cows or 1200 steers. I had help for weaning, branding and things like that but otherwise was on my own and needed help.

Where did you get your first Aussie? How did you first hear about the breed?

Saw the ad in the newspaper for a Stock dog trial in Abilene, TX. Didn't know what an Aussie or even a Stock dog was but figured it would help me do my work. When I got to the trial the first person I saw was Linda Wilson and her van full of beautiful fluffy blue dogs. I told her I was looking to buy an Aussie and that I wanted a working dog out of working parent. She pointed me toward the arena. I walked over and saw just what I needed, Windsong Rasin Cain was working. After Cain's run I went to Rick Dill and asked about puppies. Bout fainted and fell over at the idea of paying $200 for a dog! That was a lot of money on a cowboy's salary! But forked over my money.

Told Rick I did not care what sex or color, but that the pup had to work cows and not bite kids. Chris Timmons, another stock dog judge, brought my pup to his place and put her into a pen full of fluffy blue pups he had raised. When I picked her up, I did not believe she was an Aussie but just a pup they had picked up off of the road somewhere. She was a slick coated black pup with copper feet and eyebrows. Seeing my dismay Chris started telling me all kinds of good stuff about my pup, so I took her home. I had fixed her a box between my bed and the wood stove but that didn't last long. Soon we were curled up together in my bed.

Texas Sand Chase became my constant companion. I didn't have any idea about training a dog so just kept Chase with me. I fed cattle out of a pickup, horse drawn wagon and off of horseback. One day when Chase was 8 or 9 months old I was trying to move some old high headed Santa Gertrudis cows from one lot to another. They were running at me or jumping out and leaving their calves inside. I was getting hot and expressing myself rather loudly, when Chase got out of the pickup and put them where I wanted them to go. They wouldn't jump out and leave their calves in the pen with a dog in there. I thought it had to be a fluke and put the cows back here they started. Then I pointed to the pen and Chase put them in the pen with ease. I didn't know why she did what she did, but I could point and she would take care of the situation. Working stock instantly became easier.

What makes the Aussie different from other dogs that work stock?

The good ones love the work but you are the center of their life. Border Collies and Kelpies are centered on the stock.

Is it the Aussie temperament or looks that makes the Aussie special?

It is what is between the ears!

What do you look for in a puppy? What do you consider the ideal pup?

I try to look for a bold but thinking pup. One that is not afraid but looks the situation over. And of course likes me. That said, the thing to do is probably reach over into the puppies, pick up the one that appeals to you and walk away. You have just as good a chance that way of picking an excellent pup.

What do you consider the ideal age for starting a pup on stock? Do you start on sheep? Do you ever use any other stock, like ducks or goats, to start your pups?

I have started dogs as young as 5 months and as old as 7 years. But on the average I would say wait until the pup is at least a year old. He has to have the maturity to take correction. Before that time no matter what happens, when you catch the pup you have to tell him he has just done the most wonderful thing on earth. Even if he has just finished eating a sheep! I use goats or sheep. Ducks are too fragile and pups are rambunctious. Even though my first few years training dogs were on cattle, I now like to have some control before I put my pup in harm's way on cattle.

How do you raise your Aussies? Are they house dogs or kennel dogs?

The very best dog is your constant companion but most of mine are raised in big pens. They get lots of people contact as I exercise them twice a day. When I am working outside they all also shadow my every step. I think the key is human contact and respect. The pup must love you enough to want to please you and respect you enough to put your wishes before his.

How important is the relationship between an Aussie and its person?

It is the whole ball of wax

Do you let your pups follow you around when you are doing chores?

Yes but I keep them safe from harm.

When do you like a pup to show interest in stock? Does it matter? Is there an age where you would start to worry if you hadn't seen any interest yet?

I like the pup to be aware of stock at an early age. He doesn't have to start trying to work just be aware. I would worry if the pup isn't turned on by a year of age.

Is there an age when an Aussie is too old to start on stock?

No as long as the dog is physically capable. Just like with us it is hard to teach an old dog new tricks!

What sort of stock do you use in the beginning? How many?

Depends on the pup. If he is super aggressive, I use 2 goats in the round pen. If he is iffy I might let him work with another dog on 50 or 60, 5- to 8-month old kids.

Do you use a round pen? If so, at what point in training?

To start, because I can protect the stock in the round pen. I am out in the open as soon as I know he is not going to eat something. Also I am no longer able to chase a pup down in a larger area. The round pen is a wonderful tool. Any time I am having trouble with something I'll go back to the round pen to work things out.

Do you ever use an older dog to help with training? If so, in what way and for how long?

Yes, especially when I need to turn a young in training dog on or if he needs encouragement and back up. Usually with at least 30 head of goats or broke sheep in a large area.

I remember one time I had a Red Baron son about a year old who was a bit scared of cows. He wanted to work but lacked the courage. I was on the Williams' ranch in Montana. Betty was moving cows up to a high pasture with Red Baron and I was on a 4 wheeler following along behind with my pup I called Monster. Monster would run toward the cows then run back to me over and over, each time getting closer. I started watching Red Baron who had his eye on my pup. Whenever my pup would approach the herd, Red would drop back until when Monster finally got up the courage to get close, Red was right behind him, backing him up. Monster won every battle! And from that day forward he was a cattle dog. A note about a thinking dog: Red was a great dog that used his head to take care of a situation where he knew a pup needed help. Not a word was spoken the entire time. All of my current dogs have Red somewhere in their background. Dogs like this should not be lost to our breed.

You can't leave a young dog with an older dog too long because he will learn to mind the older dog not you.

What do you like pups/dogs to know before you introduce them to stock? Do you teach any commands off stock?

Yes I teach "down, stop and come" off of stock. They also usually know when I am unhappy or they are doing something wrong. An "Ah Ah" is a no word. I talk to my pups a lot as they are growing up. Their vocabulary will eventually be around 60 words.

But by the same token I do not expect any kind of obedience, not even a response to their name for about 3 to 4 weeks of work. They are learning to use their minds to control stock not obedience. I use a pressure/release type of training.

Do you ever use any tools when training, like a long line or a stock stick?

Yes I use a 6-foot leash and a cane pole about 7-feet long with a white bag tied to the end of it, though I have been known to throw just about anything that makes a noise between a dog and the stock to widen them out. Never could use a long line because I got tangled up in it myself!

What do you like to see in an Aussie in its first few sessions on stock? What would tell you that it is a good prospect?

A sense of group, some feel for the flight zone and strength on the head (self-confidence to boss stock). It is a plus if the dog will heel but it is not necessary.

Can you describe the best pup you ever started? What made it special and where is it today?

It would be the dog I am working now, Billy, now 7. I started using him at 5 months. He is the strongest dog on the head I have ever worked yet has the sense to be kind to his stock. He will stand calmly nose to nose with something until it turns off of him, but if it is aggressive it gets a nose bite. I started using him so young because he was so easy. He wanted to do what I wanted. I call him my Grandma dog. So the characteristics he had as a puppy where devotion, self-confidence and biddability.

Today he rarely leaves my side and does all my work from bringing in stock (sometimes with new babies), holding them off of the feed trough while I pour out feed, to bringing them to me for worming etc, to washing the nose and bottom of the bottle lambs. I have 2 bottle lambs at present. One has done well from the beginning but the other had to be force fed milk and would only take about 1/3 of what he needed to survive. I was about to the point of giving up on him when I let Billy do his thing while I was trying to feed him. Billy washed him from one end to another and the little thing started nursing for the first time. Now the two lambs follow Billy anywhere. By the same token this can be irritating. Billy will not hurt a baby and if he has raised them they remain babies to him. So moving them somewhere often takes more time than I want to spend! But he gets the job done.

Tell us a little about your training style. How often do you work a started dog? What skills do you like to train first? When do you move on to the next skill?

I do not train like I once did anymore. But I used to work a dog every day or at least 5 days a week. Sessions only lasted until something good happened and that could be in 5 minutes or in 30 but usually about 15 minutes. That is about the attention span you get for training. Now chores are different, you can do them all day.

The only thing I work on in the beginning is letting the dog learn to control his stock, keeping them with me and not running them past me, fetching which is the natural thing for most dogs. Teaching him where the flight zone starts and how to use it. That takes a while. I do not expect him to respond to any kind on command in the beginning. I am working on the area between the ears not on obedience. When the pup has this in his mind I start some more distance stuff, the outrun or gather along with a "stop" command, a straight into the stock "walk up" (taught on lead and if there is a secret to driving it is the secret), a "down", and a "get back" (go to the opposite side of the stock from me) command.

How do you go about teaching an outrun?

The pup already understands the flight zone of his stock so I just extend the distance a little at a time.

How do you go about teaching the drive?

That is an easy one for me probably because I worked cattle with my dogs for such a long time. It starts with stock in the far corner of a large pen. I teach a no stress "walk up" on lead straight toward them. Do not look at the dog in this exercise but keep your eyes on the stock. It is a "walk up, stop, walk up, down, walk up" exercise until you reach the flight zone of the stock. Then do whatever you were planning to do for the day. This exercise starts about day 3 of training or when I am able to work in a larger area with my pup.

Another exercise is to teach a defense of a feed pan in front of hungry stock. Get a pan, your pup on a 3 or 4 foot leash, go into the corner and kneel down behind the pan with your pup. When the stock approach, pop them in the nose and tell your pup to "watch 'em". Let him bite if he needs to but not chase them off. Just stand and watch them leave. Pups love this exercise. It teaches them to hold pressure away from you and that is driving. It is not following stock that are moving away from you, it is holding pressure away from you. You can teach a fence drive using a line, but if you do, drive in the open 4 times as much as you use the fence or you will get an odd flanking pattern.

How do you go about teaching a stop and steady?

The stop is an on lead taught thing. By steady I think you mean slow down. That is not how I use steady but slow down can be taught as an obedience command on lead, you can physically step between the dog and stock in the round pen and slow him down, or when he is walking up on stock from the other side of the round pen with pressure/release that was used to teach flight zones of stock.

How do you handle a dog that wants to grip?

No problem, teach an "out" when he comes in to grip. It is part of the fight zone thing. Also for a dog that wants to grip anything that faces him I use about 15 head of stock in the round pen, with babies if you have them. I walk the dog on lead around and around the round pen with the dog between my leg and the edge of the pen until everything settles down, the dog and stock. When everything settles down and the stock are in the center of the pen I wait until they are facing him, then stop and turn directly toward them. "Walk up" directly toward them until they turn then stand still and watch them leave. The next command is "out". Go directly away from the stock to the edge of the round pen again. You can start using directional commands here, and around the pen you go again until the stock are once again facing you then repeat.

The next step once the dog understands that he doesn't have to bite anything that faces him is to actually let him come in contact with the stock. Keep moving around and around the round pen gradually moving in from the center until you are following the stock as they move around the center of the pen. Keep things calm. The babies will get tired and fall to the back of the group. Gradually let your dog approach and get a sniff of a baby, butt first. The secret is milk manure. It is an unusual Aussie that will hurt a baby, but be careful, it does happen. All of this is on lead for sure until this point. As the dog gets calmer and calmer you will let the lead get longer then eventually drop it. You must remain absolutely calm, especially your voice and keep moving around the stock yourself, at first with your dog then as your dog starts around ahead of you. Try not to let your dog get to balance by moving yourself because he will want to come in at that point and probably bite. Catch him in the easiest way you can, very calm and love on him big time.

When do you introduce a dog to cattle?

I try to do it on broke stock out in the open with a trained dog if I have one. By dog broke I mean stock that has learned to mind a dog but haven't been abused, so that they are calm and not trying to hurt the dog. I just turn him loose and encourage him to fetch once things settle down.

Do you work for a balance between the need for obedience to your commands and the desire to develop a thinking dog?

Yes with obedience not important in the beginning.

When do you know a dog is ready to trial?

When he can be stopped no matter what and he understand how to control stock and keep them with me without running them past me. With my own dogs I usually wait until they drive fairly well to start them trialing so that once started trialing I can go through the courses/levels with no problems.

Are you a stock dog judge? What do you look for in the "perfect" run?

Ideally on ASCA courses A and B, no commands are given except drive to start and then fetch to come to the center and repen. The stock should move straight from one obstacle to the other without stopping at a fast walk or slow trot. Because there are no commands the dog is doing all the thinking and working himself. Now this is not popular right now in any venue! The popular thing is obedience only, no thinking dog, thus the new ASCA courses.

But because I come from the world of using dogs I personally feel that we are doing a great disservice to our breed or any working breed for that matter. Breeding for obedience not intelligence will change the breed to its detriment. I would have a hard time working a dog I have to tell everything to do over the hill! It is also changing the dogs in the arena. Border Collies have been bred for two things for generations, to work sheep and be obedient. So those lines of Aussies with a "touch of tail" make superior obedience dogs and will be used for breeding in the future because of their success. The old time Aussie was willing to listen to what was wanted for a while, but if it was confusing or constant commands he soon tuned you out and did his own thing or what he thought you wanted. Ranchers didn't have round pens, the dog had to figure out what was needed on his own. Dogs were valued for this characteristic.

How do you feel about trialing? Do you trial in other venues?

I enjoy trialing but don't do it very often anymore. I have finished 24 or 25 ASCA WTCH's, 5 or 6 Champions in AHBA and 3 or 4 Advanced titles in AKC. When I was training for the public I would take a dog through the WTCH then consider him a good started dog, ready for advanced trialing or using on a ranch.

I went to my first trial when Chase was about a year old. I entered everything. Cattle were easy, we did that every day but when I opened the take pen on the sheep, it was full of "deer". They jumped over me and tried to kill themselves on the fence at the far end of the arena. Chase and I had never seen sheep much less sale barn barbs! I looked down at her and she looked up at me and I thought what in the – have I gotten us into this time! It took 10 minutes to make the first two panels and I was working on the center when we ran out of time. I didn't know started didn't do the center! When they would blow by me I would point and Chase would run and shoulder them back to me. She never tried to bite one. I figured we had really messed up and was very surprised to find we were High Started Cattle and Sheep. I don't remember how the ducks were but she may have been High Ducks too.

After this trial I decided Chase needed to be "trained"! If I had left her alone she would have been fine but it took another year for her to WTCH called triple ATD then. I would try all kinds of things out on her. When she had had enough she would take my hand in her mouth and press down just hard enough to let me know she had had enough of that sh--. We would sit down under the old oak tree and think things over.

What is the most important tip you would like to give someone interested in training an Aussie for stock work?

Go to someone who understands Aussies to help you get started. The stock has instinct, the dog has instinct but we humans are sorely lacking and have to learn how to help our puppies out or even what to look for in our dog. If you are a rancher, take the puppy with you every day as you do your chores but above all keep him safe. Talk to your pup. Tell him what you are doing. Pretty soon, "get over there and lay down will also mean get over there and bring that cow to me". You have a 2 year old child with you. Even at a year of age he is still about 7 years old and must be protected. If you wanted your son to follow in your footsteps you would make his experiences positive. Do this with your pup and you will have a wonderful working companion who will seem to read your mind for the next 11 or 12 years.

ROBYN JOHNSON-GARRETT

Robyn has been raising and training Australian Shepherds since 1986, in herding, agility, obedience, tracking and rally. Her Kennel is HOF Temptation Aussies. She has bred, raised and trained multiple Australian Shepherds that have successfully competed in ASCA's Most Versatile Australian Shepherd program. Winning MVA in 2012 at the Bakersfield ASCA Nationals. She has titled six WTCHs, two Versatility Champions, four Performance Champions, and three Supreme Performance Champions from her kennel.

Robyn is an ASCA stockdog, obedience and rally judge, as well as an AHBA herding judge.
Robyn is located in Utah and offers private lessons.

To contact Robyn:

robyn@temptationaussies.com

www.temptationaussies.com

801-860-1843

How long have you been involved in training and trialing Aussies? How did that involvement come about? Where did you get your first Aussie? How did you first hear about the breed?

Although my grandfather used Aussies on his turkey farm, I knew nothing about Australian Shepherds other than they were a herding breed. I had cattle dog mixes up to the time I got my first Aussie.

I got my first Aussie from a long time friend from my horse background, Sherrie Scott in 1986. The Scotts used their dogs on the dairy. I stopped by for a visit, and she had a litter on the ground. One of the puppies literally grabbed ahold of my son's shoe and wouldn't let go. We joked that we'd have to just take her home.

I ended up taking her home. She was my first purebred dog, so I figured I'd better try to train and show her.

There was no one in the state that trialed dogs at the time, so I worked her a bit on ducks and on cattle at the Scott's dairy. None of us knew what we were doing, but when she was 18 months I entered her in her first trial - Nationals at Scottsdale, Arizona. I was so naïve that I didn't know I should be nervous about her first trial being at Nationals.

She took first place in cattle on some Brahma calves. I knew nothing. She just took them around the course by herself. Not quietly, mind you. But she got the job done. I was hooked!

What makes the Aussie different from other dogs that work stock?

The thing I love about the Aussie is the off–switch. We can hang out around the stock, do chores, and watch others work their dogs. They aren't trying to sneak off to work on their own. They truly work for the handler, and they prefer to work for their chosen person. They are great problem–solvers. I love how they have enough push to get a job done.

I have known Aussies that have put themselves in dangerous situations to save their owners from rank stock.

Is it the Aussie temperament or looks that makes the Aussie special?

I like the old time working bred Aussie's look and their temperament makes them an ideal dog for me. They will work all day, and prefer to have a daily job to do, but if there is no work to be done, they will just hang out. When the evening comes, they have an off–switch. They will find a comfy spot and do whatever you want to do.

Aussies are truly a versatile breed. I have put a lot of pressure on my dogs to do herding, agility, obedience, tracking, some conformation back in the day, and now rally. By pressure, I mean that they have had to learn to do many things, and have done everything to the best of their abilities for me. My dogs have been very successful in the versatility area earning 4 PCHs, 3 SPCH, 2 VCH. They have earned many other Championship titles in herding and agility. They have placed in the top ten at the MVA competitions at Nationals many times, and Flame won Most Versatile Aussie at the Bakersfield Nationals in 2012.

What do you look for in a puppy? What do you consider the ideal pup?

My idea of an ideal pup has changed a bit from when I was younger. My first dogs were chosen from their littermates because of their tenacity, and being the most active, hell raiser in the litter. I had a lot of success with those dogs. My last choice was a middle of the litter pup. She wasn't the most active, but she wasn't shy either. I want a confident pup that pays attention to me and what I have to offer. I want a pup that doesn't resist being held like a baby, but will only take it so long and wants to get down and play.

I usually do a temperament test on my litters and make my choice based on that and what I have observed in their day to day interactions with each other, adult dogs, people and objects in their environment.

What do you consider the ideal age for starting a pup on stock? Do you start on sheep? Do you ever use any other stock, like ducks or goats, to start your pups?

I don't know that there is an ideal age, but there is a point that the dog is ready to start. I want the dog to go to work, not go to play. The mind has to be past the puppy play time, and they have to be able to take pressure without fighting it or shutting down.

I start with sheep. I have some good ol' lesson sheep that have started many a dog. I don't prefer to start with fowl because the flapping wings can either be intimidating, or too exciting for a dog that doesn't know what it is doing.

I have taken young pups to the ducks on occasion to see the reaction. Sometimes I have brought mama along to give encouragement

How do you raise your Aussies? Are they house dogs or kennel dogs?

My dogs are house dogs with rules. I have a few dogs that would benefit from living in a kennel, I think. I have one male that pushes limits with me and the other dogs constantly. I think he would benefit from living out in the kennel, and only brought out to go to work.

How important is the relationship between an Aussie and its person?

Relationship is Key! If your dog pushes you and challenges your leadership in day to day life, you will have a hard time getting good trial work from it. You need to have unconditional obedience and respect for you as the leader. They need to trust you as well. This is not to say I don't cuddle and play with my dogs. I do. But if I ask for a behavior, they need to respond with obedience

Do you let your pups follow you around when you are doing chores?

Yes, but on a long line. I think it is very important for a dog to learn that the stock can just be around, and they don't have to go play with it. I will go out into the pasture, and weed, or hang out and we work "that'll dos" and "leave its". We may go into the sheep's bubble, and then leave with a "that'll do" a bit.

When do you like a pup to show interest in stock? Does it matter? Is there an age where you would start to worry if you hadn't seen any interest yet?

I haven't had to worry about my own dogs not showing an interest in stock. Some of my lesson people have been advised to wait a month or so and try again. I have had lesson dogs not show interest ever, and some were about two when they started to recognize the stock as something to work. Some say that dogs who turn on to their stock later make better stock dogs in the long run.

Is there an age when an Aussie is too old to start on stock?

If the mind and body is able, then no. Keeping in mind that young dogs absorb knowledge much more readily than our older dogs.

What sort of stock do you use in the beginning? How many?

I start off with three to five of my "starter" sheep. We start in a smallish arena about 80x60. At this time, we learn to go around, change direction, fetch, rate , and pace the stock. Then learn to do inside flanks and a bit of driving.

Do you use a round pen? If so, at what point in training?

I use my round pen to teach the dog to handle the pressure of a small area calmly. I also use my holding pens and alley way to help a dog handle the stock calmly, yet assertively. I may use the round pen after the dog is comfortable fetching in a smaller arena.

Do you ever use an older dog to help with training? If so, in what way and for how long?

I have brought an older dog out to help a less than enthusiastic dog get the point that the stock can be moved, or if the dog is having problems taking the stock out of corners or off fences. I don't do this often, or long. Only if other avenues have not helped the dog gain an understanding.

I do some training of outruns in an open field with other dogs and handlers holding the sheep.

What do you like pups/dogs to know before you introduce them to stock? Do you teach any commands off stock?

I want a good solid stop. A down, sit, and a stay. I want a "get back", so they release to the pressure of my body. I don't train directions off stock because I have daily access, but some of my students have been successful doing so at home using a toy lure.

Do you ever use any tools when training, like a long line or a stock stick?

I sometimes will use a long line if the dog just can't hold a "there" and is wanting to constantly go to head while learning do drive, but only on rare occasions. I do use a stock stick and a rock bottle to help enforce my body pressure and break concentration if the dog is not "hearing" commands.

What do you like to see in an Aussie in its first few sessions on stock? What would tell you that it is a good prospect?

I like to see a dog able to go around the stock in both directions, although one side is usually more comfortable than the other for the dog. I like to see a sense of group. Keep the sheep together. I like to see that the dog is bringing the stock to me. I like to see a dog that will give to pressure without shutting down or worrying.

Can you describe the best pup you ever started? What made it special and where is it today?

The easiest pup I have ever started has been Char. I don't know yet if she will be a special herding dog. She is only three and has only trialed twice at this writing. She gave me square flanks right off the bat. She was easy to teach to rate her stock and adjust her pace. She is changing a bit now. The square flanks are needing work on the go bye side, and she is also not covering her go bye side as well as I would like. Probably the best dog was Char's aunt Angel. She gave me fits as a young dog. I'm sure that was due to poor training skills. Once she figured out the game, I learned how good she was with the stock. She had a calming effect with them. She could take sheep that were running like crazy from other dogs, and within minutes they would walk quietly with her moving them around.

Tell us a little about your training style. How often do you work a started dog? What skills do you like to train first? When do you move on to the next skill?

It depends on the dog how often I work them. With the dog I'm starting now, about three times a week training. I use her for chores though. She is sorting and penning sheep and taking them out of the pens for students to work.

I like to teach the dog to give to pressure, learn the verbal directions, and not push the sheep over the top of me in a fetch. Once the dog can do that in a small area, I move quickly to larger areas and progress to lighter sheep until we are doing walk–abouts in the field with the sheep being held to me, but not being pushed over me.

We also work small outruns in first the small pen, then the arena and then the field with the sheep being held by another dog or set on hay.

We learn inside flanks, back in the small pen, by bringing the dog to me and sending the dog past me with a verbal and stick to go around the flock. Then I progress to stopping the dog at different points and having it drive the sheep away from me. Then we progress to driving further and further as the dog can handle it without going to head or charging through the middle of the stock. When we are successful in the arena driving from one end to the other and holding the line, I take the work to the field, and work greater distance from me and longer drives holding the straight line and changing the line for cross drives.

How do you go about teaching an outrun?

I start by teaching the dog to turn away from the sheep as they get up by putting body pressure on the dog. I start this is in a small area with heavy sheep that won't run off. If the dog is having a hard time releasing, I will put the sheep into a corner, so I only have to work a small part of the circle to get them to release. When they give to the pressure and turn away, I take the pressure off and walk away from the stock letting the dog find balance and do a short fetch. Again I make the progression from a small area with heavy sheep where I can control most of what is happening, to a larger area with heavy sheep to progressively lighter sheep and more distance, to working in the field with room to do large outruns holding the arc all the way around.

How do you go about teaching the drive?

We learn inside flanks, back in the small pen, by bringing the dog to me and sending the dog past me with a verbal and stick to go around the flock. Then I progress to stopping the dog at different points and having it drive the sheep away from me. Then we progress to driving further and further as the dog can handle it without going to head or charging through the middle of the stock. When we are successful in the arena driving from one end to the other and holding the line, I take the work to the field, and work greater distance from me and longer drives holding the straight line and changing the line for cross drives.

How do you go about teaching a stop and steady?

Down, sit, and stand or stay commands are taught away from the stock. I may take my young dog to do chores and ask for the commands with the stock around. I teach the stop first by using an alley way or hallway. Sending the dog back away from me and asking for a lie down. Then I take frontal pressure off the dog and ask for a walk up. If the dog comes too fast, I turn toward it and put pressure back on, releasing when I get the walk. I add the walk or steady word when the dog is actually doing a nice steady walk, thus associating the behavior with the word. Then add sheep to the alley way ask for the same thing. When you are getting it there, take it to the small arena and ask for the same thing. In the beginning, I ask for a down when both the sheep and me are at the fence so they can't get past me. I want the dog to trust that everything is under control. The sheep aren't getting away and they can trust me in asking for a down.

For the steady work, I do walk–abouts with the sheep. If the dog is pushing them past me, I turn and put pressure on the dog until the dog is giving me a steady and is keeping enough distance that the sheep aren't putting me in the sheep blender.

How do you handle a dog that wants to grip?

It depends on the grip. I don't want to lose grip on my dogs if they need it. If they are doing fly-by body bites and or wool pulling, I will reprimand with my voice and body pressure letting them know that was not acceptable work. If they continue, they leave and go to their crate. Usually the fly–bys or break–throughs are indicative of frustration. So you have to think about why it happened and make adjustments.

When do you introduce a dog to cattle?

Fairly early in their careers. When they are still fearless and agile enough to avoid danger. After directions are learned on sheep. A parallel drive is good to have as well.

Do you work for a balance between the need for obedience to your commands and the desire to develop a thinking dog?

Yes, I try to be quiet on my walk–abouts, and most of my drive work. If the dog loses sheep, I send them to figure out how to bring them back. After a few times of losing them, they are usually more careful about keeping the group together and stay off the group better. If I happen to send them on the other side of the draw, however, I want the dog to learn to take the command even though it goes against his instinct to release the pressure side. I also want the dog to obey a stop or a call–off no matter what is happening. This is a safety issue for the dog and the livestock.

When do you know a dog is ready to trial?

I keep telling myself I will wait with this dog until it is trained for advanced work before I take it to its first trial. That would be ideal.

So far, I haven't been able to do it. Poor judgment on my part. One day I will keep to my word and avoid the temptation to enter the local trial "to show my support" or to enter nationals "because it won't be so close to home for a few years." I love to trial more than I love chocolate. Both are very hard to resist.

Are you a stockdog judge? What do you look for in the "perfect" run?

I am an ASCA and an AHBA stockdog judge. The perfect run would be watching a dog taking its stock through the course calmly. The handler allowing the dog to work with minimal direction. Not to say the dog is course trained, but is taking control of the stock and moving them with quiet confidence.

I have a hard time with micro managing the dog ie. downing and drifting, or placing the dog, The worst is downing the dog and the handler doing the work themselves. How do you give a dog points for that?

How do you feel about trialing? Do you trial in other venues?

I do like to trial. I trial mostly with ASCA. It is a long drive to get to AHBA trials, so I seldom go. Maybe this young dog I have now will inspire me to make the drive.

The day to day training and general work with the dog is the best. Watching the light bulb moments, and just hanging out with the dogs.

What is the most important tip you would like to give someone interested in training an Aussie for stock work?

Find a trainer whose training and demeanor you admire. Ask questions, read books, watch videos, and watch others work their dogs. Handle livestock yourself with no dog. Observe the livestock outside of the arena as well as when they are being worked. Talk to seasoned livestock people about how to read the stock. See if you can learn to read them.

Go to all the clinics and seminars you can. You can always take something back from each seminar. Even if your brain isn't ready for what they are trying to teach at the time, at one point you will remember what the clinician said and say "AHA!" "Now it all makes sense."

I have some great influences in my life from clinicians. Kathy Warren, Jerry Rowe, Betty Williams, and Steve Shope are some that I have taken their teachings into my training.

Each of these people will recognize what they have taught me in what I have written today. I have been very lucky to live in the same state as Wade Carter. I could watch his quiet way of handling his dogs, and how well he was able to read the livestock. Watching some of the best handlers can be a great learning process and give you something to strive for.

Your dog is only as good as his instinct and your training will allow. Don't get mad at the bad dog, get mad at the hole in your training and fix it. Herding trials are a sport. Enjoy the ride.

DEVONA MYRICK

I have always been an animal love since a small child. Which could explain a lot about why I am in the Aussie world. I grow up as an Army brat, moving frequently and making new friends often. Graduating in 1973 wanting to be a physician or vet I settled for LPN school and began my journey in nursing. Married a guy from High School, had two beautiful children and divorced at a young age. Life had it's ups and downs but I returned to RN school graduating in 1994, this opened many doors for me in my profession. In 1997 I met Bob Myrick and we were married. Bob introduced me to his Aussies and I have been hooked ever since. We trained, went to clinics and practiced a lot. I had several dog before I got my Cisco who taught me more than any human about stock and working them. Cisco and I started trialing when he was 10 months and went to Finals when he was not quit two. He was an awesome dog. We did everything we could compete in: post advance, ranch trial, ranch dog certificate and lots of course A and B. I have since worked many dogs and trailed on courses C, D, E, F and Farm Trials. I have received help from many a great handler, working other breeds and handling others dogs. Dogs are like people they are all different, learn different and see things different. They fear and trust like humans and love deeper than humans could imagine.

My first love is horses and much of what I learned of pressure and release came from working horses. I tell Bob if someone had told me working a stock dog was just like working a horse I would have gotten all this three years earlier. I became a Stockdog judge in 2009 and enjoy judging but working full time as a Director of Surgical Services at the University of New Mexico takes up a great portion of my time. I usually take two to three judging assignments a year until I retire which will not be soon. I am in school for my Masters in nursing and have 40 years in nursing this year. Wow where has the time gone!

To contact Devona:

truegritfarm.devona@gmail.com

How long have you been involved in training and trialing Aussies? How did that involvement come about?

I have been in training and trialing since 1998. Bob my husband got me interested when we got married in 1997. He had three aussies at the time allworking dogs. I had never been around the breed and found them to be very loyal, hard working and great companions.

Where did you get your first Aussie?

My first Aussie came from a breeding Bob had out his two best dogs.

How did you first hear about the breed?

Through Bob, when we were dating.

What makes the Aussie different from other dogs that work stock?

Aussies are a loose-eye worker for the most part, for this reason they can work in close area like a take pen or pens in general. They are fetching dogs as a rule but can be taught to drive; they have a great sense of group.

Is it the Aussie temperament or looks that makes the Aussie special?

It is both, Aussies have great temperaments and looks!

What do you look for in a puppy?

I look for that pup that is confident and curious. Balance on their feet and people oriented.

What do you consider the ideal pup?

One that has the looks and brains that make it stand out above all the rest. Most pups are cute as we all know but there is always that one that stands out, confident, good looking and smart. I play games with pups to see how long their attention spans are, if they are scared of new objects or curious and if they follow objects that move.

What do you consider the ideal age for starting a pup on stock? Do you start on sheep? Do you ever use any other stock, like ducks or goats, to start your pups?

The age depends on the pup, some are ready as early as 3-6 months to expose to stock, some as old as 1+ years. Training should start after some ground work as happen with the pup like a down, come or "that a do" commands. I start in the round pen with dog-broke sheep/goats but advance to lighter sheep once the dog is handling well. All basic commands and training can be taught in the round pen but I take pups out of the round pen to fetch stock to train them how to cover stock better and fix their own mistakes. They do chores such as moving stock from the field to the round pen and back out to the field.

How do you raise your Aussies? Are they house dogs or kennel dogs?

My pups all start in the house to learn house manners young. Our dogs are inside and out in their kennels. We rotate our dogs in the house and travel with them so that they understand the rules. We teach them to go to the bathroom on command when traveling.

How important is the relationship between an Aussie and its person?

Most important! To have a great working relationship the two most trust each other and work as one which is of the most difficult relationships to have. Humans want to control and we fight with dog who wants to control the stock.

Do you let your pups follow you around when you are doing chores?

Absolutely! This is the best way to start with a young pup to teach him routine.

When do you like a pup to show interest in stock? Does it matter? Is there an age where you would start to worry if you hadn't seen any interest yet?

It is great if they show interest at 12 weeks or so but some will show interest at 8-12 weeks, then nothing until months older. Others are very serious intense workers from a very young age like three months. I like to see strong interest by 6-9 months. If a dog is not showing any interest by one year I start to worry some; if by two I figure it is not going to happen.

Is there an age when an Aussie is too old to start on stock?

I have known dogs that were not started until 8 years old and did very well. By ten years old, however, I would consider them too old. This is when we retire most of our dogs.

What sort of stock do you use in the beginning? How many?

Dog-broke goats or sheep, about 3-5 head. If the dog is very strong and too strong for goats or sheep we have started them on dog broke cattle but very few.

Do you use a round pen? If so, at what point in training?

Yes I use a round pen to introduce stock to a young dog it give you a more controlled area. Starting in the round pen does not mean that you cannot move to a bigger area if the dog is under control and listening well. They have to respect the stock and handler. I use the round pen to teach basic work then move to a bigger area returning to the round pen to re-enforce things when they seem confused or not clear.

Do you ever use an older dog to help with training? If so, in what way and for how long?

If I have a dog that is not turned on to stock very well I will use an older trained dog to move stock around to see if we can get more out of the younger dog but only for a time or two. I have used this with cattle mostly to help build confidence in the younger pup.

What do you like pups/dogs to know before you introduce them to stock? Do you teach any commands off stock?

I teach all commands off stock in hopes it transfers over once they are on stock and it does in most cases. I teach the down, sit, stay, go by, way to me, get back and that will do. I start with a 10 week old pup moving through these as the pup gets one.

Do you ever use any tools when training, like a long line or a stock stick?

I do use a stock stick all the time, and a long line when applicable (mostly with driving)

What do you like to see in an Aussie in its first few sessions on stock? What would tell you that it is a good prospect?

I like to see a quiet worker who is off their stock and fetching the stock to me; keeping it together nicely. Sometimes this will take a few sessions but you can see it through each session. A good prospect is one that is thinking on their feet, watching to see where you are, and going controlling the stock with little to no help from you.

Can you describe the best pup you ever started? What made it special and where is it today?

Best pup I ever started was my Cisco, he was a natural balance dog, gave to pressure, and respected his stock and handler. He taught me more about herding than any human could. We learned together how to move and hold stock, pen, and release pressure. He wanted to please more than live. We were together day and night working on our GA farm. He was not a very strong cattle dog but we could get the job done with time. He died at age 11.

Tell us a little about your training style. How often do you work a started dog? What skills do you like to train first? When do you move on to the next skill?

I like to train using pressure and release. When starting a dog I like to work 3 times a week if time allows. Like I have stated before, I start the ground work young away from stock so that when we enter the round pen the pup knows the commands even though they may not respond to them at first on stock. When putting a dog on stock the first few times I try to just see what the dog is going to do and protect the stock if needed, letting the dog think or respond to its natural instincts. From here I try to enter the scene and work with the dog to move the stock using the stock stick and commands to change the directions. I work for only about 5 minutes start with then increase as the dog can handle and holds their attention to the stock. I start to push the dog out early in training and ask for the down also. When the dog is going to stock respectfully, listening to the down and taking it I start the circle game to teach directions and the out/get back.

How do you go about teaching an outrun?

I start this in the round pen but move to a bigger area when the dog is being responsive to down 90% of the time.

How do you go about teaching the drive?

In the round pen standing against the fence having the dog take an inside flank picking up the stock and driving it away from me, this is also how I teach the inside flank of course using a down to stop the dog when he is wrong then ask them to move again.

How do you go about teaching a stop and steady?

This is something I work on from a pup with the stop. When they are doing something that is not allowed I tell them to stop this usually transfers over in the working but sometimes not. The steady is a little more difficult but I have used a long lead for this depending on the dog for both the steady and stop.

How do you handle a dog that wants to grip?

No different, you never want to take the bite out. I won't let my dog abuse stock but I do not discourage the bite at the start of training.

When do you introduce a dog to cattle?

When they appear to be able to handle the pressure of training on sheep or goats. I wait until they are at least a year and half old but there again it depends on the dog.

When do you know a dog is ready to trial?

When they are listening, handling their stock with respect and are solid on their directions and a down. I have waited until they are driving some and using inside flanks.

Are you a stockdog judge? What do you look for in the "perfect" run?

Yes I am a judge. I am not sure there is a perfect run but the perfect run one be the one where the dog picks up the stock quietly, establishes control and moves through the course with little or no problems. Not being to pushy, barking too much and using appropriate bite if needed. Few commands from handler with good team work.

How do you feel about trialing? Do you trial in other venues?

I love to trial and hope to do more of it in the coming years! I tried AKC years ago but time does not allow for all venues. I plan to do AHBA this year and maybe some field trialing locally.

What is the most important tip you would like to give someone interested in training an Aussie for stock work?

Be patient, find a good trainer to help you that you trust and like and remember why you wanted to do this.... It is for fun!

ROBERT MYRICK

Bob Myrick was born (1958) and raised in rural Georgia. I always loved animals and was active in 4-H with my dog and horse events. Once grown, I helped several cattlemen work their herds, and bought a pup from one of them for my son and soon bought another from out west, and have enjoyed working with the Aussie ever since. I worked closely with animal control and the sheriff's office when stock was loose since they learned I had good dogs, and could gather and pen most anything. Before moving to NM in 2008, we facilitated and provided stock (ducks, sheep, and cattle) for many of the trials in Ga. We had a herd of about 40 Piedmontese cows and really have missed them since moving. We now have a nice home and a few acres in NM, where we have our horses, and a few sheep for training the dogs. We are currently caring for cattle for a friend on land that is leased mainly for the opportunity to work our dogs, and help others work theirs. I enjoy working cattle on horseback with my dog about as good as anything. I am an ASCA stockdog judge, but do not participate in other venues other than to help at them. I am not a fan of obedience stock work. My preference is to allow the dog to "gather and bring" on their own without a lot of commands. I love the Ranch trial program, but am disheartened that the cost prevent many from being offered especially since ASCA does not recognize this type of event for their "finals" program. I am currently considering the AHBA venue, but am still undecided as to how involved I would want to be. I am not very competitive, and just enjoy low stress stock work.

To contact Bob:

truegritfarm@gmail.com

How long have you been involved in training and trialing Aussies? How did that involvement come about?

Since the late 1980's, I think 1988. I knew a cattleman in GA that used them on his ranch. I helped him some and was amazed at how the dog would know what to do without being told.

Where did you get your first Aussie? How did you first hear about the breed?

Refer to #1, I bought my first Aussie from him.

What makes the Aussie different from other dogs that work stock?

IMO more sense. More confidence. Of course there is so much variation in breeding programs, and I am referring to a very few Aussies. I have seen several "other" breeds that do a good job, and I have seen many Aussies that could not do a good job. It is genetics and environment that determine how well the dog will work stock.

Is it the Aussie temperament or looks that makes the Aussie special?

Again, there is a lot of variation in breeding programs, but MY Aussies have an excellent temperament, and look good IMO. It is the "adaptability" of the Aussie that I love.

What do you look for in a puppy? What do you consider the ideal pup?

I first look at the temperament of the Sire and Dam; then I want to study the working characteristics of the Sire and Dam. As far as "picking" out a pup out of a litter, I have not seen anybody that was successful consistently at forecasting what a particular pup will be like. I do however "pick" my pups based on their attentiveness, and socialization abilities with dog and man. I also believe environment plays as big a part of how a dog turns out as genetics.

What do you consider the ideal age for starting a pup on stock? Do you start on sheep? Do you ever use any other stock, like ducks or goats, to start your pups?

I don't think you can determine an age. I have had pups that were ready at 3 months to work cattle, and I have had pups that at 3 years were not ready. I usually feel that if a dog is not showing interest at 1 year, they are not going to be a great herding dog. I do expose my pups to ducks just to see how they react, and never want to put them in a position that would hurt their confidence. Stock will vary per pup for me.

How do you raise your Aussies? Are they house dogs or kennel dogs?

Ideally, my Aussie would live with me 24/7. Realistically I have to work and leave them in a kennel while I work to keep them safe and out of trouble. I am trying hard to get my numbers down so as not to have any dog that "lives" in a kennel. The more time one spends with the Aussie, the more rewarding the experience will be, and I think this would be true with "other" breeds as well.

How important is the relationship between an Aussie and its person?

Utmost! Should start out that way, and never waiver.

Do you let your pups follow you around when you are doing chores?

Absolutely! If they get too interested and cause trouble, I will kennel or chain them in a safe place.

When do you like a pup to show interest in stock? Does it matter? Is there an age where you would start to worry if you hadn't seen any interest yet?

I prefer to see interest right away, but must see interest by 1 year, or I look for a pet home for them. I have had a 3 yr old dog that was not interested in cattle that did eventually work cattle, but I just don't have that much time.

Is there an age when an Aussie is too old to start on stock?

I have no reason to start an older dog, but feel that <7 could be worked with "IF" the instinct was sufficient.

What sort of stock do you use in the beginning? How many?

Depends on the dog. I have had pups so aggressive cattle was the only way I could start them, but that is not the norm. I usually prefer sheep or goats and like to have a minimum of 5 and up to 20. Again, that depends on working style of dog.

Do you use a round pen? If so, at what point in training?

Yes, but only early or if I am having a hard time with my communication. If a dog is listening and staying off the stock, I much prefer a larger area.

Do you ever use an older dog to help with training? If so, in what way and for how long?

If you have a "really" good dog, it is a good idea to let a young dog work with the veteran to learn how it is done. I would not suggest working multiple dogs on a small number of sheep unless one has no interest and the object was to "turn on" that dog. I have had several pair that worked cattle really well, but I have also put 2 dogs on a herd and quickly saw it was a bad idea, again it depends on the dogs.

What do you like pups/dogs to know before you introduce them to stock? Do you teach any commands off stock?

Come! I like to have a stop (I don't want to down them, but often that is the only alternative). At first I just want to see how they respond to the stock, and that they are not going to "eat" the stock.

Do you ever use any tools when training, like a long line or a stock stick?

Again, it depends on dog. I do use a stick as an extension of my arm as a visual, and will use bottle with rocks if need be to get attention.

What do you like to see in an Aussie in its first few sessions on stock? What would tell you that it is a good prospect?

I love to see a young pup go to balance, and respect the perimeter. I do not like to see splitting even at an early age.

Can you describe the best pup you ever started? What made it special and where is it today?

Wow, that is hard. I have been very fortunate. I have had several really good dogs that were better at one thing or another, but I can't really say my best pup was______.

Tell us a little about your training style. How often do you work a started dog? What skills do you like to train first? When do you move on to the next skill?

How often to work a dog depends on their maturity and my schedule. Unless a pup is showing signs of not wanting to work, I don't think you can work them too much. I have never worked a pup as much as I would have liked to. As far as my training style, I do not train for an arena. I like to see the pup "think", and figure out "how" they would control stock. I do not train my pups as much as I learn to work with them. I do take control to keep my stock safe, but I let my pup fetch (something they understand) longer than most. Once they really understand how to control stock, then I will attempt to "drive", but will not take their confidence away to do it. I really have little use of a drive, as I have to get up to a gate to open it, and I prefer my dog taking care of the other side.

How do you go about teaching an outrun?

Typical, block and send. I cannot say I have ever mastered this, only because I have not figured out how to get some of them to "release" prior to letting them go to balance. The tighter they are at the top, the tighter they will be on the back side. The best way I have found is to get the idea in the round pen, then get out in a larger area. Send the dog. At the very point they start to slice in, correct them and call them all the way back and resend. This is ONLY after you have taught them what you want and they are not doing it.

How do you go about teaching the drive?

I use a modified fetch first, and increase the distance gradually so they really don't even realize they are driving. I then reward by letting them fetch back.

How do you go about teaching a stop and steady?

I will have a down prior to going to stock. I also try to have a "stop". I use a "slow" command and apply pressure with my body, and if they don't respond, I will give the "down". Once I give the "down", that is what I want! Once they have the slow, I will ask them to "stop", and praise them big for it when I get it. I usually use a fence to help control the stock so the dog does not have so much to do when "training" this. Never say "steady, steady, steady" while a dog is running amuck, for that only teaches them "NOT" to pay any attention.

How do you handle a dog that wants to grip?

That depends entirely on if it is an appropriate grip or not. If I am asking them to move stock, and they need to grip to get movement, I praise it. If stock is moving and the dog wants to grip, I need to be there between him and the stock. If I can't be there, I am on the way, and growling so he knows that is not acceptable behavior!

When do you introduce a dog to cattle?

Depends on cattle, and dog. Normally around a year.

Do you work for a balance between the need for obedience to your commands and the desire to develop a thinking dog?

Yes! If I give a command, I want it to be paid attention to. I try hard to not give a command if it is not needed. This also depends on if I am "training", or doing chores. If I am training, I expect my command to be done! If I am doing chores, sometimes I allow some mischief to keep from losing livestock.

When do you know a dog is ready to trial?

Depends on your goals. I prefer to have a dog ready for Open and Advanced prior to trialing, but many times I have got started titles strictly on instinct with a come and stop the only commands my pup knew.

Are you a stockdog judge? What do you look for in the "perfect" run?

I am a judge. I want to see "quiet confident control of livestock". The start of the run should be smooth, and a fluid motion throughout the run. How a dog approaches stock determines how the run will go. I want to see a dog "in contact" at all times. I want to see enough confidence to only apply enough pressure to get stock moving, and then a release. The perfect run will need almost no commands. The dog will rate itself and read "balance", and maintain it. On a started run, I could care less if a dog drives.

How do you feel about trialing? Do you trial in other venues?

I am losing interest in "trialing". I love working stock, and doing "practical" work, but I in no way desire to have an obedience dog that I work stock with. I wish our trial program were more "practical" oriented like the farm and ranch trials. ASCA does not recognize those programs for Finals competition because there are many "WTCH" dogs that cannot do that type of work. The other problem with those programs is cost. Most clubs cannot afford enough stock to put on those type trials, and most competitors have little desire to pay the required fees since they render no "finals points". At this point, I have not trialed other venues, but have interest in cattle trials from horseback. Since I no longer own a herd and work on a regular basis, I have doubts that I will ever be a real competitor.

What is the most important tip you would like to give someone interested in training an Aussie for stock work?

First decide what your goal is. Are you interested in winning in the trial arena, or actually working stock? If a dog does not have instinct to go to balance, get another dog, or just be happy with a pet. Learn to work with the dog, as most of the time they know how to handle stock better than we do. Only apply enough pressure to get the desired response. SHUT UP!!! Do not give verbal commands until 100% correct. Incorrect commands are very detrimental to training! If it is not fun, quit until you can figure out how to make it fun for you and the dog. It is our responsibility to make the task successful. If we set up for success every time, we will be successful. If things fall apart, back up to the basics and BE SUCCESSFUL, and take a break. Use a video camera to see what is happening. No one can tell you as much as a picture! Look at your work and think what should have been done better. Don't blame the dog, almost always it is our fault! Enjoy your dog, ALWAYS!

Thank you for purchasing this book. If you enjoyed it, please leave a review on Amazon so others may be encouraged to read it as well. If you have suggestions for people to include in Volume Two, please email me their names and contact information!

Laura's Bio:

Laura has been herding for 9 years and has trained, trialed and/or titled a variety of dogs, including Briards, Bergermascos, Pumis, Border Collies, Aussies, Kelpies, Shelties, Collies, Corgis, ACDs, Rotties and even a Greater Swiss Mountain dog. She is both an AKC Herding Judge and an AHBA Herding Judge. Laura owns a Briard, 6 Border Collies, 6 Aussies, 2 Kelpies and an Anatolian Shepherd.

She owns (trained, trialed and titled) the first Herding Champion in the El Paso/Las Cruces area (and the second, third and fourth), the first Double-Herding Champion in the area (and the second, third and fourth), and the first dog to earn an AKC Herding Excellent title in the area (and the second and third and the first to earn 2 HX titles)! Her Border Collie, Star, was the subject of an article in the BCSA "Borderlines" magazine in 2012 and her older Border Collie, Joker, was featured in the Aug/Sept Veterans edition of the "Borderlines" as Joker earned his second HX at the age of 11 (fewer than 100 dogs have accomplished that in the history of AKC) in 2013. In 2014 Star did what less than 10 dogs have ever done in the history of AKC, and that is earn an HX on Cattle at the age of 10 or over.

Laura lives in Chaparral, NM, between Las Cruces and El Paso, TX where she owns and operates Take Pen Herding.

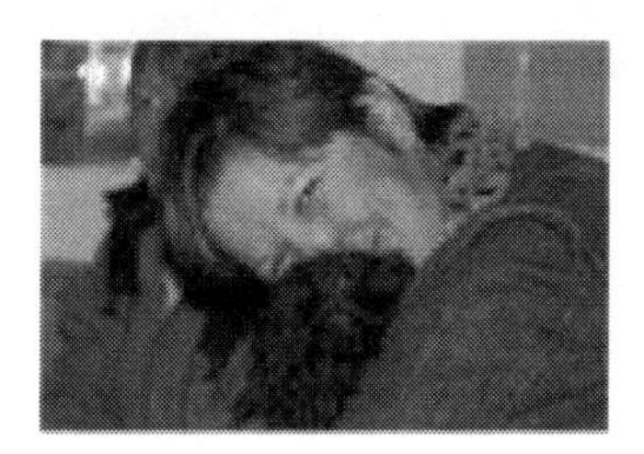

10999968R00033

Made in the USA
Lexington, KY
03 October 2018